DESTINATION
HOPE

ENDORSEMENTS FOR *DESTINATION HOPE*

Everyone makes plans for the future, but what do you do when everything explodes? You reach for *Destination Hope: A Travel Companion When Life Falls Apart*. Written by Marilyn Nutter, who suddenly lost her husband, and April White, who recently had a rare genetic illness invade her life, readers cross seven mile markers, intertwining their stories and others who survived with God's help, getting to the other side of a broken heart.

SHARON BALDACCI
Author of *A Sundog Moment*

Destination Hope: A Travel Companion When Life Falls Apart* is a gentle, thoughtful guide through the rocky terrain of life. No matter what hardships we face, discover transformational, personal stories that will resonate deeply, inspiring you to hold hope because spring is coming and new life will again take root in your heart.

PAMELA PIQUETTE
Executive Director and Co-Founder of Chronic Joy®

Has your life taken a turn you were not expecting? Then this book, *Destination Hope: A Travel Companion When Life Falls Apart* is just what you need! Marilyn Nutter and April White take you on a journey to find hope when your life is rocked by an unexpected event: loss of a spouse, illness, wayward children, loss of a child, and other disappointments. I love how these two authors share from their own life experiences, how they found hope in the midst of difficult, life-changing circumstances. This book gave me fresh perspective on finding hope in the disappointments in my own life. A must-read!

CRICKETT KEETH
Author of *On Bended Knee: Praying like Prophets, Warriors, and Kings*

A great read for the road trip of life. Marilyn and April are your wise—and wounded—travel guides for the unexpected detours in life including widowhood, chronic illness, stolen identity, empty nest, prodigal children and more. They offer hope and healing from Scripture and the victorious testimonies from numerous women along the winding way.

JAMES N. WATKINS
Award-winning author and speaker

Destination Hope: A Travel Companion When Life Falls Apart is a "must-read" invaluable guide, offering hope and sound wisdom for our unpredictable, individual life journeys. Written by two of the wisest tried, tested, and true women of God—April White and Marilyn Nutter—you will see how each author poured out beautiful transparency. Like two best friends who've trailed the hard ground before us, April and Marilyn, seem to gently take us by the hand and lead us toward God's heart for healing.

LATAN ROLAND MURPHY
Award-winning author of *Courageous Women of the Bible*

But what if the pain persists? What if the money is not provided? What if the loss is irrevocable? For many, the journey of life includes devastating detours and rigid roadblocks. The question becomes, *how does a believer keep going in her new normal?* Authors Marilyn Nutter and April White are no strangers to rocky paths, but they remind us to keep putting one foot in front of the other in their new book *Destination Hope: A Travel Companion When Life Falls Apart.* What a valuable guide for all those uncertain times of *recalculating.* The poet Christina Rossetti once said, *"Does the road wind uphill all the way? Yes, to the very end."* Through such sobering reality, Nutter and White sit with us in our pain and offer biblical teaching and many stories of people just like you and me who have embraced the hope of God's presence, power, and provision. I heartily recommend this practical and inspiring book for anyone who feels your life is falling apart; which is, of course, many of us on this perilous and glorious journey.

LUCINDA SECREST MCDOWELL
Author of *Soul Strong* and *Life-Giving Choices*

MARILYN NUTTER and APRIL WHITE

DESTINATION
HOPE

a travel *companion* when

life falls apart

AMBASSADOR INTERNATIONAL
GREENVILLE, SOUTH CAROLINA & BELFAST, NORTHERN IRELAND

www.ambassador-international.com

Destination Hope

A Travel Companion When Life Falls Apart

ISBN: 978-1-64960-109-4
eISBN: 978-1-64960-159-9
Library of Congress Control Number: 2021942167

Cover Design by Hannah Linder Designs
Interior Typesetting by Dentelle Design
Digital Edition by Anna Riebe Raats
Edited by Megan Gerig

Scriptures taken from the Holy Bible, New International Version®, NIV®. Copyright © 1973, 1978, 1984, 2011 by Biblica, Inc.™ Used by permission of Zondervan. All rights reserved worldwide. www.zondervan.com The "NIV" and "New International Version" are trademarks registered in the United States Patent and Trademark Office by Biblica, Inc.™

Mile Marker designed by Brgfx / Freepik

AMBASSADOR INTERNATIONAL
Emerald House
411 University Ridge, Suite B14
Greenville, SC 29601, USA
www.ambassador-international.com

AMBASSADOR BOOKS
The Mount
2 Woodstock Link
Belfast, BT6 8DD, Northern Ireland, UK
www.ambassadormedia.co.uk

The colophon is a trademark of Ambassador, a Christian publishing company.

DEDICATIONS

To my late husband Randy, who took me on an adventure of a lifetime, who was my biggest cheerleader, and who encouraged me to step out and attend a writers' conference that was life-changing. Even now, I see your smile and hear your applause. Till we meet again. ~Marilyn

To my parents, Roger and Liz, who taught me the power of listening, the importance of unhurried back porch conversations, a full cookie jar for the neighborhood children, and whose actions taught me the significance of dispensing hope amid life's challenges. ~April

TABLE OF CONTENTS

MILE MARKER THREE
EXPLORING HOPE IN UNCHARTED TERRITORY. . . .71

MILE MARKER FOUR
SHIFTING PERSPECTIVE TOWARD HOPE. 101

ACKNOWLEDGMENTS

MARILYN

With thanks and appreciation to those who have shared in my personal journey and in writing *Destination Hope*: The women who responded to surveys and wrote their stories, sharing their hearts and life interruptions, offering hope to others. Fellow writers who critiqued our work, offered suggestions, and most of all encouraged and prayed us through this project, especially Tammy, Jeannie, and Katy. My church family at Life Fellowship, who in their shock and grief held me up in weeks, months, and years in prayer. My special friends waiting for me with open arms when I relocated to Greer. My prayer warriors—too many to mention by name. Your faith and encouragement enriched me. My family for their prayers, encouragement, and support, and though we see an empty chair at every dinner, have learned laughter in love. My precious grandchildren who always make my cup run over and give me more glimpses of Jesus each time we meet. April White, from that first email and meeting by the grand fireplace at the Cove, we connected, then prayed, planned, wrote, and revised. You taught me much more than the craft of writing. Ambassador International team and Megan Gerig, our editor, for embracing our project and sharing hope to those whose lives have been interrupted. Most of all, I thank my Lord Jesus, Who from the first moment of loss, gave amazing grace, mercies, and faithfulness that have never stopped. From the beginning, You told me You were creating a new script for me, and You have created one that has exceeded what I imagined.

"Now to him who is able to do immeasurably more than all we ask or imagine, according to his power that is at work within us, to him be glory in the church and in Christ Jesus throughout all generations, for ever and ever! Amen."

Ephesians 3:20–21

ACKNOWLEDGMENTS

APRIL

This book is a work of my prayer warriors and friends. Together, we spent countless hours of conversations over cups of coffee, carpool lines, and kitchen tables. How do I find the words to frame my years of gratitude in various seasons when it is overflowing?

To Jesus, I would have given up on me a long time ago. Thank You for Your long-suffering nature, daily mercy, and unending grace. To Marilyn, your friendship is proof of God's divine timing. Thank you for faithfully reminding me, "I am the Lord; in its time I will do this swiftly" (Isaiah 60:22b). To Ambassador International for embracing and launching this project of hope to others knocked off course. To the women who allowed us to share their stories, thank you for leading others with similar struggles toward a destination of hope. To the faithful readers of first my Christmas letters then my blog, I am thankful to each of you for reading my work, encouraging, and challenging me to continue to write. To Sara for suggesting I start a blog and giving me the courage to step out into deep water. To my friends at Radford Baptist Church for holding us up in prayer when we were paralyzed by my sudden illness and uncertainty. To Meg, whose genuine friendship left an embroidered image on my heart. To Brenda Gay and the women at Shepherd's Gate, you wrapped me in wisdom and encouragement through a difficult season of life. God continues to answer your prayers. To Michelle, Susan, Karen, Vie, Cindy, Barbara, Amy, and my Circle of Sevens gang, you pushed this project toward publication while it was in seed form and prayed over me in the process. I treasure your friendship. To Andrew and Rachel, thanks for enduring each stage of the writing process, my illness, and my moods. To Chris, for over two decades and two children, and for telling me to write.

"I thank my God every time I remember you."

Philippians 1:3

INTRODUCTION

Dear Friends,

We wrote this book with you in mind. We know what it's like to go through hard times and life-altering circumstances. Although we have encountered separate and different challenges, we meet similarities in our journeys. Often in our writing, we pictured you, your struggles, and your disappointments. We get it.

Destination Hope: A Travel Companion When Life Falls Apart is arranged in seven mile markers. Like a mile marker along a highway, these markers note places in your unfamiliar journey, remind you of your progress, and offer direction as you meet hope in each place.

Any traveler knows that rest stops provide places to refresh, replenish, and rest. Our Rest Areas in *Destination Hope,* shown by a bench image, come at strategic places as you walk toward hope. Take as much time as you need to linger at these Rest Areas and ponder each reading. Reflect and journal on not only what you've lost, but also what you've learned and gained. Use this time to regroup and rebuild your stamina, to work through grief, or to seek a new perspective. Like any trip, we take postcards from racks to remind us of places. We have included postcards at the end of each narrative and in the back of the book for further encouragement as you travel. These postcards are also available to download from our websites, www.MarilynNutter.com and www.AprilDawnWhite.com.

Reflect, rest, and journey toward hope. We're traveling with you.

Warmly,

Marilyn and April

> *"Friendship is born at that moment when one person says to another: 'What! You, too? I thought I was the only one!'"*
>
> C. S. Lewis, *The Four Loves*[1]

MILE MARKER ONE

FINDING HOPE IN AN
UNEXPECTED TRIP

I DIDN'T PLAN THIS

I inhaled the aroma of freshly brewed coffee in the lofty library space. Colorful book spines and displays lured my senses to clasp a book and escape my current reality. Where would I like to go? I surveyed the librarian's top books for the week. I passed over the recent YA dystopian fiction and a popular self-help books and selected the novel, *Mr. Churchill's Secretary* by Susan Elia MacNeal. This historical fiction novel set in WWII drew me in. Although this is a tragic chapter in world history, I was compelled to read about a time when people had to rely on God, grit, and grace. I am usually the one who encourages others, yet I need encouragement too. Here in this library, surrounded by meticulously selected words, I knew I would find encouragement as I read how others overcame tragic circumstances. With a deep sigh of contentment, I thought, *This is my happy place.* While waiting my turn at the circulation desk, I perused a display of travel guides to local, domestic, and international locations.

A copy of the *Lonely Planet Scotland* travel guide caught my attention.[2] The sweeping lush green meadows and distant eighteenth century castle stirred a longing to see tartan kilts and bagpipes in person. Opening the cover page I read, "Your travel guide to Scotland in four easy sections.

> One: Plan Your Trip. Your planning toolkit. Photos and suggestions to help you create the perfect trip.
>
> Two: On the Road. Your complete guide. Expert reviews, easy-to-read map, and insider tips.

Three: Understand. Get more from your trip. Learn about the big picture to make sense of what you see.

Four: Survival Guide. Your at-a-glance reference. Vital practical information for a smooth trip."

Turning to the back cover I sarcastically questioned, *Okay, but how do you plan for a trip you didn't expect?* I checked out the book for two reasons. First, because my husband and I were dreaming about a European vacation with Scotland at the top of my list. Second, I wondered if the tour guide truly did provide a plan for a perfectly executed trip. And I wondered how you took a trip you didn't plan or expect.

The coronavirus has dramatically changed our way of life and sent us all on a trip we didn't plan or expect. Travel, employment, education, and contacts with friends have been interrupted. Our supermarket shopping has become a creative exercise in adapting menus to available products. Some have experienced a loss of income, health, and even the death of loved ones. Milestone markers of commencement and school activities have been knocked down and thrown to the roadside.

No one predicted or expected this detour. Our isolation and quarantine, depending on location, has affected us mentally, relationally, emotionally, and physically. Like a car broken down on a highway, we are waiting for rescue.

We wake in the morning and don't go to work. Kids are home from school. There are no sports practices to attend and no music lessons to take. We are prohibited from visiting hospitalized loved ones. This virus captured the world's attention with an unexpected pandemic of isolation, fear, and loss. Life has been interrupted and our stop is indefinite. The good news is that this pandemic, or any circumstance, doesn't stop God's promises. Hope is not quarantined.

{ "Don't see your struggle as an interruption to life but as preparation for life."[3] }

MEET APRIL: BLINDSIDED BY AN
UNEXPECTED DIAGNOSIS

Nerve endings exploded like bottle rockets as I gasped my husband's name. A heavy oppression overtook my body as, unknown to me, a rare disease crawled through my skeletal muscles. I tried to shake off the electric shocks stinging my legs, but I couldn't move. The raw tingling pain crept across my face and shoulders.

Like Superman exposed to kryptonite, I was immobile.

My facial muscles would not contort my brow into the question embedded in my mind: what was happening to me? Lyrics to an old hymn waltzed past the question. A voice, perhaps mine, perhaps God's, assured me, "It is well; it is well with my soul." Peace replaced the question lodged in my thoughts. I whispered aloud, "Lord, I don't know what this is, but I trust You."

Months later, I met a neurologist. "Try to smile for me."

I couldn't.

Placing his hands on my face, he said, "Raise your eyebrows."

I couldn't.

My skeletal muscles displayed a classic myotonic state of periodic paralysis. Tears leaked down my face, and I lacked the strength to wipe them away. Apologetically, I muttered my desire to be normal again.

"What is normal for you, Mrs. White?" the doctor asked.

Inhaling deeply to summon extra strength, I responded, "Normal is working and feeling like a productive member of society and being physically active. Normal is volunteering at my kids' school, playing the violin, playing ball with my kids, attempting to keep my house straight, cooking meals for my family and for others. Normal for me is talking with the other moms at carpool instead of staying in my car alone afraid that if I stand I will fall flat on my face. Normal is not feeling isolated.

"What is normal for you, Mrs. White?" My mind pondered the doctor's question for days. Curious, I opened the Bible app on my phone and performed a keyword search for the word "normal" in the New International Version. Normal: No results found.

My days of thinking I am "normal" are long gone. The medical alert bracelet dangling from my wrist indicates my disease state and serves as a permanent accessory. I am not in control and there is no fix. Even though I desire to participate in some of my "old-self" activities, I realize my desire to be normal is a warped self-image with no Biblical backing—that I did find in Scripture, as well as reminders that we are never in control. I have a Creator Who made and sustains me. My new desire is to fulfill God's purposes for me in this unique, difficult, and rare position. Dare I say privileged? I couldn't say it at first, but I can say it now. That perspective evolved in my journey.

My local neurologist finally tentatively diagnosed me with Hypokalemic Periodic Paralysis, and after a year of genetic testing, multiple nerve conduction tests, EMGs, and a referral to Duke Medical Center his diagnosis was confirmed.

Hypokalemic Periodic Paralysis is one of several Periodic Paralyses, rare genetic disorders affecting as few as 1 per 100,000 people. The symptoms of periodic paralysis include unexplainable muscle weakness, loss of strength, and numbness of limbs, hands, and/or face, and random partial or full-body paralysis. These attacks can last as little as a few minutes to as long as days.[4]

As part of my new "normal" morning routine, I contort my face and shift my body to determine the severity of symptoms of this illness. Each day I wonder, will today be a "good" day? Then I pray, "Lord, I love You. Lord, I trust You. I trust Your plan. I trust Your provision for me. I trust in You perfect timing. Amen."

By the grace of God, new medications, and physical therapy, I can go most days with little assistance. Each morning I drag my little red chair (my sacred place of time with the Lord) adjacent to God's throne. Knees touching with the Almighty, I receive an infusion of hope directly from my Creator. While Hypokalemic Periodic Paralysis has hijacked by body, it cannot hijack God's presence or my praise.

> Trials and detours are an invitation to a front row seat to God's faithfulness.

Like Horatio Spafford, I have learned to say, "It is well, it is well, with my soul."[5]

There is no cure for my disorder, and I have not miraculously been healed, but since my diagnosis, I've had a front row seat to God's faithfulness. He continues to astound me by revealing His purposes for my life, His provision for my needs, and His faithful presence. God's chronic presence is present in my chronic illness. I have daily hope in this unexpected journey and cling to the promise found in 1 Peter 5:10, "After you have suffered a little while, [Christ] will himself restore you and make you strong, firm and steadfast."

What incident or experience blindsided you? Do you relate to April's desire to get back to normal? What are your thoughts about 1 Peter 5:10?

"God's chronic presence is present in my chronic illness."

April White

MEET MARILYN: BLINDSIDED BY SUDDEN WIDOWHOOD

I clutched my husband's suitcase but not his hand. My cross-country return flight home would be a solo trip. Randy and I traveled to Idaho mid-December 2011 to spend the Christmas holidays with our oldest daughter and her family. Our youngest daughter, Kate, flew in from Charlotte and met us several days later.

My husband Randy never saw that Christmas on earth. A fatal heart attack claimed his life. With six words spoken by a physician, "I'm sorry. He didn't make it," my life fell apart. A morning that began as a woman married for forty-two years and four months, ended with my new label: widow. My vision for life in my sixties had been trips, conversation, ministry, trips with grandchildren, walks, meals, all with my husband. But these plans were now shattered like broken glass.

As I waited in line at the airport check-in counter, I rehearsed the shocking events: ER, life-flight, surreal, blindsided, and unthinkable. Our family's words spoken at hearing the news, "There must be some mistake," thickened the fog of grief. The first four words described our immediate reaction; the fifth, was unfortunately, not true.

My son-in-law changed our return flight home and canceled my husband's ticket. I traveled home with only his suitcase. I wondered who took his seat on that flight? Maybe it was someone who decided to fly at the last minute, thankful a seat had opened during the busiest travel season of the year. What a contrast—my tears and a stranger's relief.

Once home, while we tried to make coherent funeral plans, the hours and days blurred as a haze around me. Who plans a funeral around the holidays?

But we had to. The memorial service was beautiful with the tributes and the presence of supportive friends and family who came from hundreds of miles away. Days later, when everyone went home, my real grieving and mourning began, not just in my aloneness, but in beginning the myriad amounts of necessary paperwork. You can't die in America without paperwork.

As I sat one evening, staring into space, the foggy contrasts of the week appeared front and center:

- A diseased heart in life versus Randy's healthy heart in heaven.
- My role of wife versus my role of widow.
- My grief versus a stranger's gratitude for an available seat.
- A family Christmas celebration with children's laughter versus a Christmas turned into pain and tears of grief.
- A full life with my companion versus loneliness in a quiet house.
- Speaking "we" versus speaking "I."

In lucid moments, I prayed and wondered what lay ahead in my new single life, a life I felt ill prepared for. The days and months that followed sometimes contained two steps forward and three steps back. Challenges and decisions occupied time in ways that were unfamiliar. I cried. I cleared my throat when I answered the phone at ten because I hadn't spoken to anyone since I woke at seven.

{ This life change will not destroy me. I can have hope. I will live in hope. I am hopeful. }

I knew from observing other widows that not all days would be hard. The days would grow different; maybe not always better but different. I knew I would always miss my husband and best friend. I knew I wouldn't always shed tears, and one day, I would laugh. I knew I was leading a changed life, and I was sad and lonely.

I also knew I had hope, and one day, I would live there. But at that moment and in the months to come, I followed the words of my pastor, "Marilyn, grieve and don't rush the grief." My journey moved gradually toward finding purpose in a new season. Like April, I live with hope.

I reflect though I no longer use the pronoun "we,"
I am not alone. God's presence never leaves me;
He accompanies me.

Grieve and don't rush grief.

Marilyn Nutter

WHAT? I LANDED WHERE?

"I'm going to be a Nonni!" I was thrilled when I learned my youngest daughter was expecting her first baby. She eagerly shared photos of her bulging belly and each milestone of the baby's development. When Kate and my son-in-law hosted a gender reveal party, a tiered cake revealed blue icing. A family phone tree called relatives with the baby boy news, and shopping for all-things-boy began in earnest.

When news of pregnancy is announced, we often wonder what the baby might look like. Will he or she have Daddy's curly brown hair? How much will he or she weigh? Will he play baseball or like to play with Legos? Will her hair be curly or straight? Will she wear the baby sweater hand crocheted by my grandmother for me? We escape into dreams about and for them. Parents place preferences on gift registries and shop for nursery furniture. We pray and plan, and after several months of preparation and eager anticipation, labor pains begin and delivery is imminent.

In her essay, "Welcome to Holland," Emily Perl Kingsley likens the planning process of pregnancy and parenthood to planning a trip to Italy.[6] Eager moms-to-be, like Kate, search the internet and may read *What to Expect When You're Expecting* and other pregnancy books just as one would purchase guidebooks to an upcoming trip to Italy. Kingsley extends her analogy and describes the scene of a plane taking off and landing in Holland. The flight attendant's announcement comes as a surprise. She repeats it to herself. Holland? Her ticket clearly said Italy and she'd made plans accordingly. She read the guidebooks and looked forward to the sites and Italian food. No, this is not a mistake. She is told her baby is born with Down syndrome. Kingsley has landed in Holland. Unprepared for a child with a disability, she has to shift her thinking to life in Holland. She has had a major change of itinerary.

Kingsley candidly shares the pain of missing Italy because it is a significant loss of a dream. She looks at others enjoying Italy and she isn't there. Her limitations make living in Italy impossible. However, in Holland, she meets new friends who also unexpectedly landed there, and over time, she begins to accept a different life at a slower pace—a life counterculture to the world around her. Holland brings challenges and a new way of living, but it also brings new discoveries, opportunities, and joy; some are uniquely hers and priceless.

Her honesty resonates with those of us who have experienced an unexpected itinerary change, perhaps the death of a dream or a major life alteration. We may not have a child with a disability, but her story of altered plans marked with unexpected change echoes in our hearts. Some women planned:

- To be married . . . but decades later are single.
- To possess job security . . . but are disappointed, stuck, or furloughed.
- To have children . . . but wrestle with infertility.
- To live happily ever after . . . but go through a messy divorce.
- To have children thrive . . . but one struggles or is a prodigal.
- To experience the ideal family . . . but some are estranged, relationships are tense, or family members live at great distances.
- To have friendships . . . but meet loneliness, betrayal, or bullying.
- To be confident . . . but meet an identity crisis.

Yes, we travel to unexpected places and live in plans we didn't make or anticipate. Perhaps we temporarily visited those places and are now on another itinerary. Some find support to manage living in the new location, others find resolution and move on, still others struggle and wonder where and when the new road will emerge. Expectations continue to be unmet.

For some, however, the unexpected place is permanent. There is no opportunity to leave or fix your loss. It's not easy. The partly cloudy weather report is the daily forecast. Do you desperately want to know you are not alone—that someone understands?

We all meet itinerary changes. Life seasons bring changes, but some are permanently life altering. They are accompanied by lifestyle adjustments, changes in relationships, and perhaps a struggle with identity. Emotions rise and fall, new challenges surface, and loss is present. Like wearing a lanyard for a group tour, loss can mark us and become our identity if we allow it.

Kingsley learned landing in Holland offered new experiences, opportunities, and connections. It wasn't an easy journey with a fairy-tale ending. Her Holland was permanent. She couldn't get over it but had to live in it. Emily Kingsley's story is an example of a major life-altering event and seismic shift in expectations. Her story is one of the many narratives you will read in *Destination Hope.* In our journeys we don't deny where we are. We need to mourn our loss—our disappointments of where we were and wanted to be—but we can learn and grow. We can reach for hope and find our "Holland" may offer something we would have never otherwise seen.

What is your "Holland?" Write about your itinerary change. What are your thoughts, emotions, and challenges? Have you found new experiences, opportunities, or friendships? What have you learned about yourself?

"When we are no longer able to change a situation, we are challenged to change ourselves."

Victor Frankl[7]

MEET NAN: DECIDING TO HOPE IN BROKENNESS

My first book, *The Perils of a Pastor's Wife*, was waiting for production with Lighthouse Publishing of the Carolinas.[8] Our love story and our testimony of finding God's faithfulness and His presence in the lonely fires of ministry filled the pages. Then my world fell apart.

Still, to this day, it takes my breath away to think about the revelation of my dear husband's affair with a very close friend. Shock and disbelief ran rampant through my heart and across the mountain community in which we live.

I immediately contacted my publisher and told him I would not/could not market this book because it felt like everything within its pages was a lie. He encouraged me to write an additional chapter to explain what happened; thus, chapter ten, "I Didn't See It Coming," was born from a place of raw pain and emotion.

The chapter begins, "I felt the warm drip of tears pooling on my nightgown as my heart tumbled onto the page. Sweet sister, never could I have seen this coming. Never. Ever. David and I have experienced amazing love throughout our marriage. We've been a team in everything. In our small mountain community, our names are synonymous with one another. Always. David and Nan. Together.

Now it's over. I've never been so broken. So fragile. So alone. Isn't that ironic? I began this book by exhorting you to realize that somewhere, somehow, someone knows what you're going through. Now I'm the one in need. I need your love and your prayers as I share with you the end of my marriage, at least as I have known it for thirty-one years."

I wrote this chapter four times before I could rid myself of the poison. I was determined not to disgrace the man I had loved for thirty-one years. As I wrote and rewrote these pages, the Lord revealed many mysteries He keeps hidden in the Secret Place for those who dare to seek Him with their whole hearts—lessons of rebellion, lessons of redemption, and the one I needed the most: lessons of forgiveness. I certainly wasn't able to forgive in that moment, but His love and attention to imparting His truth to my heart set me on the journey toward forgiveness.

I was required to forgive, but not to trust, and certainly not to reconcile under these circumstances. For two-and-a-half years I mourned. Over and over I rode the tumultuous waves of sorrow, searching my heart, wringing my hands, tangling and untangling my thoughts. The man I had loved all these years was dead—I did not know the man he had become.

God sustained me with His faithfulness. He bathed me in His grace, and by His hand and by His strength alone, I was able to forgive so that my heart could be free again. I thought I had learned all there was to learn about grace during this time of brokenness, and then the unthinkable happened.

In October 2016, David showed up at my house. He was completely homeless, just a shell of a man. He had no job, no phone, no car, no home, no extended family that wanted him, and he had walked for two days to get from the foothills of North Carolina back to our home in the mountains.

I turned him away on that Saturday morning and told him he wasn't welcomed. I sobbed as I watched him walk away with his head down, all his earthly belongings in a backpack slung across his slouched shoulders. That night as our son was going to work, he passed his dad walking along the highway. It was October and getting cold, so my son picked him up and brought him home.

David could barely speak. I called the homeless shelter, but there was no room. David begged us not to take him to the hospital, so after an emergency family meeting, we decided he could stay in an extra bedroom upstairs until we could stabilize him. The next morning, we met with a crisis counselor who designated me as his caregiver.

The first several weeks, David was so suicidal we could not leave him alone. He was in counseling two times a week, heavily medicated—it was awful. The tension was horrible. The awkwardness between us was horrendous. It's hard to find words that adequately describe how painful and difficult this situation was.

Yet, I knew I was doing what the Lord had asked of me.

As hard as this was, it would have been even harder to know that David had died alone under a bridge. Without us, he would not have survived much longer. This, I am sure.

Weeks turned into months, and before we knew it, months turned into a year and a half since he had first knocked on my door. God was working during this time. We were becoming friends again. I no longer felt like I was going to throw up if he accidentally brushed up against me. It was still hard to look him in the eyes, but progress was slowly but surely being made.

As time marched on, the kids and I noticed that something was not right with David. He began falling, frequently. He had difficulty following our conversations. He wanted to help us by washing dishes, but he didn't know to rinse them. He tried to warm pizza with a paper plate in a hot oven. He didn't know the simplest of things like identifying broccoli. This man had a master's degree in theology, yet it seemed his intelligence had vanished.

Recently, this precious man—this mighty man of God—has been diagnosed with a rare form of dementia: frontotemporal dementia. This type of dementia affects the frontal and temporal lobes of the brain, the place that controls our personality, reasoning, and judgment. This diagnosis explained everything! The adultery, drinking, lying, cursing—the drastic change in the man I loved.

David and I now enjoy each other's company and are growing close again in friendship. I've discovered David can still make me laugh, which is wonderful.

He is still sleeping upstairs while I sleep in my bedroom downstairs. I don't know if that will ever change—I take each day as it comes—but I do know this: the Lord clearly spoke into my spirit asking me to take care of His faithful servant until His dying day. And this I will do. By God's grace alone.

Am I afraid of the future? Sometimes, especially when I forget to think on those things that are lovely, pure, and worthy of praise. I need to be drawn back to the truth of Philippians 4:8; "Finally, brothers and sisters, whatever is true, whatever is noble, whatever is right, whatever is pure, whatever is lovely, whatever is admirable—if anything is excellent or praiseworthy—think about such things." The Lord has told us repeatedly to fear not, for He is with us. That is my sure place. I know that I know the Lord is with me, and I have really learned that His grace is sufficient. I know the future will be extremely difficult—probably more difficult than I can imagine—but I know the amazing grace that has sustained me thus far will be waiting for me in the tomorrows. I'm standing tenaciously on that promise.

You can find more about Nan Jones in the resources.

"Walking by faith means being prepared to trust where we are not permitted to see."

John Blanchard[9]

MILE MARKER TWO

LOOKING FOR HOPE WHEN LOST

WE'RE IN THE SAME STORM BUT IN A DIFFERENT BOAT

The beginning of 2020 ushered in a world-wide storm. The coronavirus storm, affected every town, village, and hamlet in the world. Regardless of our geographical location or nationality, all of us have been swept under by the storm surge of a viral outbreak. As tragic as the coronavirus pandemic of 2020 was it has brought the world closer together. A world map dotted with COVID-19 cases showed marks on every continent including Antarctica.

Faith and hope are on the forefront of people's hearts. People sing on balconies to encourage each other and resolve, "We will get through this." Television networks are airing the salvation message of Christ and encouraging interviews of clergy without reservation. Hope is in the center of the coronavirus. Christ is in the eye of the storm.

While we were all facing the same storm, we were not all in the same boat. Like an unexpected hurricane, no country could prepare for the widespread contagion rate and resulting death. This pandemic wiped out the global infrastructure of health resources and finances. Our world was on lockdown. People were forced to stay home. Schools were closed for the academic year. Non-essential businesses were forced to close. The global economy tanked. Some families were fortunate to work from home during this lockdown, the social distancing mandate not affecting their paycheck; however, millions of others found themselves hanging by a thread, furloughed from work with no return date.

The notion of same storm but different boat is applicable to those facing hard times. What is the name of your boat? Perhaps your boat has several names. Marilyn, a widow at retirement with grown children, understands grief and the loss of her husband. But her situation is different from a young widow with littles at home. A person who has lost her job and needs to relocate for work has a different boat compared to someone who finds a job locally. Playing financial catch-up from a falling stock market is different at age thirty than age sixty. Each different boat, however, whittles down to grieving over the loss of our former familiar life.

The storm is not a one size fits all. Losses vary in magnitude from person to person. When and how they occur in our life affect our perspectives. Even family members who experience the same loss, such as the death of a loved one, are impacted in different ways. Marilyn's grief is different from her daughters' grief. Even her daughters grieve in different ways for their dad.

There are multiple meanings to the word loss. "Loss" may be visible or invisible, silent or troubling. Loss may be current or something we carry for life. Whether our loss is prominent or invisible, current or not, it is complicated. It may be remote or unfamiliar to you, but bigger than life for me. Like two houses side by side in the same storm but one is destroyed and the other intact, the storm affects us in different ways. Both owners heard and saw the effects of the hurricane. They were both scared for their lives as well as their property. Perhaps one home was occupied by adults and another a family with three children. Waiting through that hurricane looked different. Heading outside after the hurricane revealed different emotional, personal, and material responses and effects. Loss is personal, important, and unique.

In Mark 4:35–41, we read about Jesus inviting His disciples to get into a boat and row to the other side: "That day when evening came, he said to his disciples, 'Let us go over to the other side.' Leaving the crowd behind, they took him along, just as he was, in the boat. There were also other boats with him. A furious squall came up, and the waves broke over the boat, so that it was nearly swamped. Jesus was in the stern, sleeping on a cushion. The disciples woke him and said to him, 'Teacher, don't you care if we drown?' He got up, rebuked the wind and said to the waves, 'Quiet! Be still!' Then the wind died down and it was completely calm. He said to his disciples, 'Why are you so afraid? Do you still have no faith?' They were terrified and asked each other, 'Who is this? Even the wind and the waves obey him!'"

Are we afraid, anxious, and restless like the disciples? Regardless of the name of our storm, Jesus desires to be in our boat. When Christ steps into our boat, He changes the atmosphere of our environment and invites us to His peaceful presence. He calmed the raging storm with two words "Be still." He is eager to do the same in our life today.

On another occasion, look at Peter (also known as Simon) and see what Christ can do when He steps in our boat. Peter recognized the power of Christ stepping into his boat. Peter, a professional fisherman, returned to the shoreline defeated with empty nets. Jesus, waiting for Peter on the shoreline, asked to step into his boat. Peter complied and Jesus used Peter's boat to preach to the crowd. The acoustics of the water amplified Jesus' message. Afterward, Jesus suggested Peter try fishing again, this time with Jesus in the boat. I imagine Peter rolled his eyes when he said:

> "'Master, we've worked hard all night and haven't caught anything. But because you say so, I will let down the nets.' When they had done so, they caught such a large number of fish that their nets began to break. So they signaled their partners in the other boat to come and help them, and they came and filled both boats so full that they began to sink" (Luke 5:5–7).

Whatever storm we endure, we can have hope. Holocaust survivor, Corrie ten Boom, lived through the most horrendous of storms. She was part of a working-class family in Amsterdam. When the Nazis invaded the Netherlands, the ten Boom family became active in hiding Jewish refugees. Their home became known as The Hiding Place, with a secret room behind a false wall that could hold six people. On February 28, 1944, a Dutch informant betrayed the ten Boom family and the Nazis arrested the entire family.

Corrie was initially held in solitary confinement and three months later had her first hearing. She and her sister Betsie were sent to a concentration camp and then to a women's labor camp in Germany. They held worship services after a day of hard labor, using a Bible they had smuggled in. Betsie's health continued to deteriorate, and she died on December 16, 1944, at the age of fifty-nine. Before her death, she told Corrie, "There is no pit so deep that He [God] is not deeper still." Corrie was released fifteen days later. Afterward, she discovered her release was due to a clerical error, and that a week later, all the women in her age group were sent to the gas chambers.[10]

After the war, Corrie returned to the Netherlands to set up a rehabilitation center for concentration camp survivors and unemployed Dutch. In 1946 at a speaking event, she recognized two Nazi soldiers who were stationed at her concentration camp, one of whom had been particularly cruel to Betsie. After the speech, Corrie ten Boom, met and offered forgiveness to the weeping soldiers. Corrie pulled the strength to forgive from this verse, "And hope does not put us to shame, because God's love has been poured out into our hearts through the Holy Spirit, who has been given to us" (Romans 5:5). She went on to travel the world as a public speaker, appearing in more than sixty countries. She wrote many books during this period, including *The Hiding Place* and *Tramp for the Lord*.[11]

Corrie ten Boom died on her ninety-first birthday in 1983. She left an incredible legacy of trust and hope in God in the most devastating circumstances. Christ was in her boat and with her in the Nazi concentration camps. She said, "In order to realize the worth of the anchor, we need to feel the stress of the storm." Whatever storm we face, God promises to never leave us nor forsake us (Deuteronomy 31:6). Whatever storm we endure, we can have hope. Christ is our anchor in the storm (Hebrews 6:19).

What storm are you facing? Have you ever felt like you have been going through the motions but have come up empty handed? What would happen if you invited Christ into your boat? Can you think as Peter did, "Master, if You say so . . ."?

"In order to realize the worth of the anchor, we need to feel the stress of the storm."

Corrie ten Boom

CIRCUMSTANCES CHANGE BUT GOD DOES NOT

-APRIL-

A mystery illness began moving my world into confusion and uncertainty years before my medical team labeled that illness. A genetic mutation hid in my DNA, waiting for hormonal changes in my forties to trigger a rare chronic illness. Suddenly, the life plan I had carefully constructed since college derailed into an abyss of unknown. All the while, God was planning to interrupt my personally scheduled life with His bigger plan. God entrusted a microscopic genetic mutation, a pre-destined change, to alter the course of my life and faith and that of my family and onlookers.

For the first few years, my mind couldn't process the changes. My questions dangled unanswered and became more tangled as new challenges arrived. My scientific and analytical mind craved order and reason. I wondered, why this, and why now? One question I did not ask was "Why me?" I've never thought the Christian life should be free from trial. When this illness began, I thought, "Oh, this is going to be my burden to bear *now.*" I am acutely aware that everyone is dealing with something, visible or invisible.

Prior to this illness, God had delivered me from postpartum depression, a miscarriage, and a baby who screamed every night for twelve weeks straight (colicky doesn't even begin to explain it). Not only did I have an account of the God of Moses parting the Red Sea, I had a personal account of God holding me up during critical times of life. I hoped this trial, like the others, would run for a designated time with an expiration date.

But this time, it was different. Unlike previous situations, my illness forced me to surrender control. I was unable to work, to help provide for our family, and to help myself. Surrendering total control to God was the simplest and scariest decision I've ever made. Ultimately, it came down to one question: Do I trust God? Yes or No. I circled *Yes* on the invisible test and gave my worries about my health, family, finances, etc. to Him. Over time, God met my needs but on His timetable. God daily reminds me when the time is right, He will make it happen (Isaiah 60:22). Over the course of this book, I will reveal His specific answers, not always a solution or fix, but answers to my prayers.

> Surrendering total control to God was the simplest and scariest decision I've ever made.

During this time of abundant change, words from Malachi 3:6 were a balm for my aching soul: "I the Lord do not change." I scribbled in my prayer journal, "Lord, I need to savor the words of Your promise. God, over the past year, so much of my life has changed; I desperately need the reminder today that You do not change. So much has changed, and I need You. My health has changed—from healthy to a rare genetic disease. My mood has changed—from happy to bouts of depression, anger, and dark thoughts (for which I sought counseling and medication). Simple abilities have changed—some days I lack the strength to lift a coffee mug or walk without assistance. My career has changed—I am no longer the pharmacist I trained to be. My income has changed—I have not worked since January 2016. My priorities have changed—rest and recovery are on my to-do list. My posture has changed—my head droops and silent tears fall freely. But Lord, You do not change. Please help me. Amen."

My favorite attribute of God is His immutability. He is the same yesterday, today, and tomorrow (Hebrews 13:8). While somewhere in my genetic code a mutation occurred in my DNA, God does not change. He does not have bad days, bad weeks, or hormonal changes. God is always good, constantly kind, and loving. He is long-suffering toward His children and full of tender compassion. He brews a fresh batch of mercy every morning. Great is His faithfulness (Lamentations 3:22–23).

God stepped into my world of chronic illness with His chronic presence. My muscle strength fluctuates and attacks of uncontrollable paralysis surface unannounced, but He remains unchanging in His chronic compassion and love toward me. All is not well with my body, but it is well with my soul.

What changes have you faced? While our circumstances may change, we can cling to our unchanging God. How does this knowledge alter the perspective of your circumstance?

"I the Lord do not change."

Malachi 3:6

MEET ERIN: DISCOVERING OPPORTUNITIES AND TALENT FOR A NEW SEASON

In 2009, Erin Odom and her husband lost their jobs with a missionary agency. Saddened and ashamed, she and her husband chose to carry this secret alone. As missionaries, they relied on God's provision through the giving of others. The termination of their ministry weighed like a lead apron on their hearts, and they questioned if their ministry was an epic failure to God, themselves, and others. Embarrassed by their termination and struggle, they became increasingly isolated.

Not every burden we experience requires an audience. Sometimes our burdens are so personal and private that we can't bear to share them. This is the lesson Erin and her husband learned. While they could have shared the gritty details of their termination with others and requested prayer, they chose to walk through this alone with God. As missionaries, the Odoms learned to journey with God and trust in Him alone. They learned the art of seeking Him first rather than seeking the distracting opinions of others.

Erin describes their faith as an integral part of their journey. "We learned to trust God to provide for every need. We had little money. It has helped me realize we can do everything "right," and life can still feel like it's turning out opposite of what we've dreamed. God is still faithful and sovereign, and He directs our course."

After the loss of their careers and expectations and hopes for a future on the mission field, Erin adjusted her skills and learned to create more income from home to help support their family. Erin wrote articles for a local newspaper and began a blog. It was not an overnight solution, but gradually, her blog, The Humbled Homemaker, led to contracts for two books: *More Than Just Making It: Hope for the Heart of the Financially Frustrated* and *You Can Stay Home With Your Kids: 100 Tips, Tricks, and Ways to Make It Work on a Budget.*

Through her struggles, Erin's perspective of God changed. She believes "It has solidified [knowing] it's God, and not us, who provides for our needs." Our life may not look like what we have planned, but when we look to Him for guidance, take responsibility for what we have, and have courage, we can move forward. Our needs may look different and sometimes we don't even know what our real needs are, but God sees every one of them. Erin believes God has used her story to share and encourage others.

You can find more about Erin Odom in the resources.

MEETING AT THE CROSSROADS OF CHANGE AND TRANSITION

-MARILYN-

Change and transition meet at the crossroads of familiarity and uncertainty. I learned this lesson when I transferred from a small women's college to a state university. I planned to change colleges after my sophomore year, but I wasn't prepared for the ensuing transition.

At my former college, class registration took place in a faculty member's office. Together, we selected classes in a personal manner. However, at the state university, the school assigned me a day and time to register with hundreds of others. The registration lines were long, and I waited eight hours to complete the process. As I waited in line, I pondered the reality of my new life at a larger university. I exchanged the familiarity of a small school for an impersonal university.

My former professors knew me by name. Now entering a lecture hall with five hundred students, I was a number. I hoped I made the right decision. That day was the first page of a new chapter. I spent eight hours in a registration line, but my transition to that larger university took a semester. I often got lost on campus. Asking for help was part of the process. But along the way, I met new people and created new friendships. Eventually, I knew my way around and began to feel more at home.

Decades later, after the death of my husband, I experienced another change and transition. I decided to sell my house and move to be near family.

I interviewed realtors, assessed the cost of a move, and began purging household contents. In a new season and different house, there were things I didn't want or need. I made trips to a charitable organization with boxes of items to donate. I rented a storage unit for some items I knew I would keep but didn't want cluttering my house. I listed my house and for weeks lived in a museum, prepared at a moment's notice to vacate so a prospective buyer could visit. Did I say weeks? No, months. Seventeen. People prayed each time I had a showing. One objection was the buyers wanted a one-story house. Mine was two-story. I was baffled by the delay as I changed seasons and decorated for another Christmas. When my house finally sold and I relocated, I realized in hindsight, it wasn't about the house, the new buyer, or the house waiting for me. It was about me. God was getting me ready, without wearing a widow's cloak accessorized with emotions, to begin a new season and meet new friends. He was in the timing of the change and preparing for the transition.

In *Psalm 23: The Shepherd with Me* Bible study, Jennifer Rothschild explains, "Your Shepherd is beside you, behind you, before you, and with you all the days of your life."[12] God's presence is always with us on our paths, weaving the scenes and characters in our lives to write our stories for His glory. We are still moving forward as God continues to write our stories. The scene may have changed, and chapters of our lives might have been altered without our permission, but we can cling to the promise and be "confident of this, that he who began a good work in you will carry it on to completion until the day of Christ Jesus" (Phil. 1:6).

Those walking the taxing path of uncertainty understand the crossroads of familiarity and uncertainty. The comfort and familiarity we once experienced intersects with murky ambiguity. A change in our circumstances (loss of a dream, divorce, illness, or a job termination) may cause an end of financial stability, security, a career, and perhaps loss of identity. People don't spend much time thinking about change until a life-changing event occurs. Let's face it, future unforeseen change is not a dazzling topic at the neighborhood backyard cook-out. But many people, including the experiences of the women in this book, felt blindsided by these events and found hope waiting for them.

Our move from change to transition is not linear. We will experience detours and pitfalls along the way. There will be moments of waiting that last so long we question if we'd been forgotten. We will experience The Five Stages of Grief, denial, anger, bargaining, depression, and acceptance.[13] When we allow our heart to process these feelings, we shouldn't be surprised if these emotions reoccur. There is no time limit to our grieving.

The severity, time, and impact of the change and our readiness and willingness to embrace change determines our next steps. You may think outside the box and creatively do something you hadn't thought about before. Changes are opportunities for new beginnings. I have widowed friends who began golf lessons and a painting class. Another friend studied for a real estate license. It is not always that easy. Perhaps an illness has you sidelined or limits you. Perhaps now, for the first time in forty years, you live alone. Perhaps money is tight. Beginnings also involve new values and attitudes. It's establishing priorities and determining with purpose, what possibilities are reasonable, what you value, and what is a good fit for you.

Change and transition is a process, which is why we shouldn't beat ourselves up or expect too much from ourselves overnight. Maybe we should each wear a sign on our foreheads that reads, "Progress in Process."

-APRIL-

Hypokalemic Periodic Paralysis knocked the wind out of me like a sucker punch to my gut. Once I could catch my breath, all that remained was the hollow of a forty-year old woman with a bruised spirit and a broken heart. As I tried to regain my wits, I sensed life had somehow sped up to warp speed.

Unable to keep up, my life morphed into my favorite childhood Atari videogame, Frogger. The goal of Frogger was for the frog to hop across the street without being squashed. As the gamer progressed from one level to another, the street transitioned to a busier highway with more traffic, becoming increasingly more difficult to pass safely. Rather than hopping between cars, I jumped emotional hurdles such as my sudden health change, financial changes, and the future unknown. In the video game Frogger, fast moving traffic threatened to squash the frog.

When crisis occurs, we have two choices: to become bitter or better. Over the course of living with this illness for five plus years, I've learned that people who have never experienced my circumstances, unwillingly say the wrong things. They don't know better. In my own life, well-meaning people tried to fix me with unsolicited opinions, suggesting natural remedies, pushing their products or essential oils. One person constantly sent me messages with the name of a doctor their family member went to and now that person "is just fine." Politely, I messaged her back that I will look into it. (Interestingly, she has never checked up on me in the past five years.) Another person, who is not employed in the medical field, questioned if my illness was real because she had never heard of it. In each of these scenarios, I could choose to be bitter by their unintentional hurt or I could choose to better the world with encouragement.

Eventually, we transitioned to a new home, a new town, a new school, and a new church. The transition landed me in a place of a new Bible study, a new book club, a new small group, and new friends.

In my sphere of North America, chronic issues and suffering is the antonym of our quick fix society. Our God is long-suffering (Psalm 86:15). He prefers to take the longer route (Exodus 13:17-18) for our good, to fulfill His purposes, and to display His glory. Each morning I make the choice to be better not bitter. I recite a prayer I memorized from speaker Graham Cooke of *Brilliant Perspectives*. "Lord if you don't heal me today, then I need you to be my keeper."[14] Unable to go back in time, I pressed on into the unknown; certain God will guide my steps. "In their hearts humans plan their course, but the Lord establishes their steps" (Proverbs 16:9).

 Identify your changes, endings, and beginnings. How would you assess your reorientation and adjustments? Explain what changes in personal values, perspectives, or attitudes you've experienced. How does the illustration of a crossroads help you to process your situation?

 "Not in his goals but in his transitions, man is great."

Ralph Waldo Emerson[15]

RECOVERING A STOLEN IDENTITY

-APRIL-

In 2018, I was the victim of identity theft. The source was not through an online transaction or a lost checkbook, but the high school guidance counselor's office.

My son, a rising tenth grader, and I visited the high school guidance counselor. While he discussed course schedules, I filled out necessary paperwork: parent name, address, phone number, and occupation. Occupation. This word haunts me. For over fifteen years, I wore a lab coat, hung my license on the pharmacy wall, and displayed my Doctor of Pharmacy degree in a prominent place in our home. Today, the lab coat hangs in the back of the closet, and my diploma is stacked in the corner of the basement collecting dust and cobwebs—much like my mind during severe moments of brain fog.

The word and blank on the parent form mocked me. It demanded an answer. I left it blank. What was I supposed to write? Pharmacist with rare illness unable to work, medically retired, full-time patient, disabled, professional paper filler-outer, CEO of the family, First lady of the White house (My last name ‹wink wink›), chauffeur, home management expert, and writer. The identity thief slipped in without notice. Perhaps he hid behind the motivational posters decorating the office. Maybe he hid behind the letters that used to follow my name, April White, B.S., R.Ph, Pharm.D. That thief stole my identity.

I was proud of myself for not crying. Instead, I moved on to the remaining pages and noted emergency contact information. I returned to the occupation question and continued to contemplate what to write in the blank. However, I was distracted when my son and the counselor discussed his foreign language options. Pausing, I lifted the pen toward them and said, "You've had two years of Spanish. Didn't you say you wanted to learn German?" My son was excited to learn a new language, but he thought since he had taken two years of Spanish, he would be stuck taking Spanish III.

This made me realize that I too have a new language to learn. I must interpret lies for what they are and learn to listen to the truth of who God says I am. "The thief comes only to steal and kill and destroy; I have come that they may have life, and have it to the full" (John 10:10).

Listening for the voice of God is like learning a foreign language. I must listen, read, and practice, reciting the words of God aloud. I need to be so familiar with His words that they automatically roll off my tongue with the correct inflection and accent, as if it is my first language.

Our enemy the devil is a liar. Jesus said in John 8:44b, "When he lies, he speaks his native language, for he is a liar and the father of lies." The identity thief may lurk in the shadows of our lives, murmuring lies and doubt, but he does not have the authority to reside there. After His resurrection, Jesus told His disciples, "All authority in heaven and on earth has been given to me" (Matthew 28:18).

Just as my son recites memorized Spanish words and phrases by rote, we can repeat the truth of who we are in Christ. We can counter Satan's lies with God's truth.

In Christ we are:

- A child of God (Galatians 3:26)
- Accepted (Romans 15:5–7)
- Blessed (Jeremiah 17:7–8)
- More than conquerors (Romans 8:37)

- Chosen (Psalm 50:15)
- Forgiven (Luke 7:47–48)
- Seated in Heavenly places with God (Ephesians 2:6)
- Delivered from sin and darkness (Galatians 1:4)
- A valiant warrior (Judges 6:12)
- Loved (Jeremiah 31:3)
- Given grace upon grace (John 1:16)

I thought the enemy stole my identity, but he does not have the authority to do that. However, he is cunning enough to make me doubt God's Word, who I am in Christ, and all the spiritual blessings God wants to give. The enemy began in the garden when he asked Eve, "Did God really say . . . " (Genesis 3:1) and continues trying to cast doubt to this day. My identity doesn't rest in social media clicks and likes, where I live, or what I do. My identity lies in who God says I am. I am a masterpiece by His design (Ephesians 2:10).

Think about a time you questioned your identity. What triggered the doubt? Take a few moments to write about wrestling with doubt or lies. From the list of phrases of who we are in Christ, which resonates with you the most and why?

"When you accept the fact that your true identity includes being an overcomer, you will never settle for less than a miracle."

Craig Groeschel[16]

READING MAPS WITH INVISIBLE INK

-MARILYN-

In 2009, my husband Randy and I retired to Charlotte, North Carolina. Due to Charlotte's explosive growth, many new roads were not updated on the GPS, so the new road my husband and I traveled was not on our GPS. As we continued to venture out to explore stores and restaurants in Charlotte, the GPS tried to recalculate, but the map on the screen became a solid screen. The GPS did not recognize the new road we traveled and gave us no direction. We stayed on that road, confident we'd arrive at our intended destination, and we did.

We often feel that way about life interruptions. We didn't plan to be on the road of heartbreak, illness, or financial reversal, but we are. We had no idea that road existed for us, but we are on it and often have no direction how to proceed.

Carol went in for a routine mammogram and several days later received a call telling her to return because the radiologist saw a suspicious spot. From there, she had a biopsy, more surgery, and a road marked with treatment, baldness, nausea, and fatigue.

Kate submitted her resume, was called in for an interview, then returned for a second interview. Her hopes soared as the conversation exceeded thirty minutes and the manager gave her a tour of the building. Finally, she received a call notifying her another candidate was selected for the position, but there was good news (from the viewpoint of the employer). The company offered her a part-time opportunity with no benefits and less salary.

Laura and her husband listed their home on the market. Despite numerous showings and decreasing the asking price, the house didn't sell for two years. This caused a financial setback and altered their plans to relocate to a warmer climate. Instead, they moved to another location with a lower cost of living.

Those invisible roads are part of every life season. Children and teens are disappointed when they don't make the team or acquire the part they wanted in a school play. Student musicians aspire to make regional and state choirs and orchestras and don't see their name on the list of those who made it. They practiced for hours, but nerves, a few wrong notes, or a superior performer edged them out, and now they have a shattered dream.

With the coronavirus pandemic, high school seniors and their parents were missing the important rites of passage like prom and graduation. The school closings affected the students anxious to interview with college recruiters and sit for the SATs or ACTs. In college, friends and roommates packed their dorm rooms and said their goodbyes early. Everyone missed their freedom. Home and online instruction led to frustration and isolation. These invisible roads, the ones we didn't know existed yet unexpectedly showed up, can demoralize or strengthen us. Sometimes, we outgrow their disappointment and later embrace something better or different. Other times, these roads affect us for life.

> "If my ships sails from sight,
> it doesn't mean my journey ends,
> it simply means the river bends."
> Enoch Powell[17]

Recalculations call for adjustments and a change of plans when we are on a road we didn't intend to travel. Sometimes recalculations are voluntary; sometimes someone else writes the script. Regardless, the once-invisible road is clearly visible.

How do we recalculate? We reflect and ponder. We assess and regret. We cry and ask, "Why, how, or when?" We complain and lament. We pray and ask others. Once the invisible road with its new signs and markers is clear and we see that it will take us places, we prioritize and may set new goals and dreams. We may determine to value each day as sacred and live it fully as best we can.

How we think about, face, and address our recalculations determines our level of resolve and contentment. Perspective and resolution can lead to the scenic route and can enrich the trip with new opportunities and landmarks. Carol's breast cancer diagnosis was irreversible but resulted in opportunities to comfort two friends who years later received the same diagnosis. As it turns out, Kate's part-time job was the catalyst to enroll in graduate school. In Laura and her husband's new location, new friends were waiting to greet them. As they say, "Plan B was really Plan A in disguise."

In the moment, we may not see through tears, but the benefit of hindsight offers insight. Perhaps later, we see our growth in character during a detour may have been strength and preparation for another challenge. Change and detours may be better than our plan, and once we move through disappointment, we see it was for the best. It may be that we are at the right place at the right time, and we can candidly say, "I'm not glad it happened, I still wish otherwise, but I see it had a purpose." Sometimes a detour is a pause, and there is benefit in the waiting. Waiting well is an important something, not a nothing. We grow and assess as we wait.

In the book of Philippians, the Apostle Paul says, "I rejoiced greatly in the Lord that at last you renewed your concern for me. Indeed, you were concerned, but you had no opportunity to show it. I am not saying this because I am in need, for I have learned to be content whatever the circumstances. I know what it is to be in need, and I know what it is to have plenty. I have learned the secret of being content in any and every situation, whether well fed or hungry, whether living in plenty or in want" (4:10–12). Paul acknowledges finding contentment was a process, not an overnight event.

Whether you have a momentary setback, a major disappointment, or a serious life-altering experience, and are recalculating, Psalm 62:11–12 offers a traveling companion of confidence: "One thing God has spoken, two things I have heard: 'Power belongs to you, God, and with you, Lord, is unfailing love'" and "You reward everyone according to what they have done."

 What did your invisible map and detour hold? How are you recalculating today? Perhaps you are waiting for the next step to take. Take time to read and reflect on the encouraging truths in these passages:

"Do you not know? Have you not heard? The Lord is the everlasting God, the Creator of the ends of the earth. He will not grow tired or weary, and his understanding no one can fathom. He gives strength to the weary and increases the power of the weak. Even youths grow tired and weary, and young men stumble and fall; but those who hope in the Lord will renew their strength. They will soar on wings like eagles; they will run and not grow weary, they will walk and not be faint" (Isaiah 40:28–31).

"So do not fear, for I am with you; do not be dismayed, for I am your God. I will strengthen you and help you; I will uphold you with my righteous right hand" (Isaiah 41:10).

"I will lead the blind by ways they have not known, along unfamiliar paths I will guide them; I will turn the darkness into light before them and make the rough places smooth. These are the things I will do; I will not forsake them" (Isaiah 42:16).

 "I am not saying this because I am in need, for I have learned to be content whatever the circumstances. I know what it is to be in need, and I know what it is to have plenty. I have learned the secret of being content in any and every situation, whether well fed or hungry, whether living in plenty or in want."

Philippians 4:11–12

MEET JENICE: EMBRACING HOPE IN PARENTING A CHILD WITH DOWN SYNDROME

After the birth of my firstborn son, Sam, the doctors told me he had Down syndrome (Trisomy 21). Although the doctor had advised me to undergo prenatal testing due to my maternal age of thirty-seven, I did not. Since my husband and I would not consider abortion, we viewed the prenatal testing as unnecessary.

My initial reaction was shock. I felt overwhelmed as to how to care for him. Here I was not only a first-time mother but the mother of a child with Down syndrome (DS). I felt helpless and terrified. I knew our lives would never be the same. My son would be different from our friends' children and our lives would be different from theirs.

I remember thinking a week or so after we brought Sam home, we were lucky he had no heart health issues that often plague children with DS. But my mind wandered. If God gave us Sam, what else would happen? The foundation of my life had turned upside down. I began to wonder when the next shoe would drop. I was a new Christian, and though I had passionately pursued my faith and loved the Lord, I was scared. Every dream I had about being a mom and raising a child was gone. Although I was falling in love with our son, I was grieving the loss of the comfortable life I had and the dream of a "perfect" baby who would grow to become an accomplished and successful man.

My family was supportive and loving. My dad, who had never appeared to take a strong interest in his grandchildren, surprised me. Immediately, he showed interested in Sam and his development. Others were also helpful and tried to be positive and show their love for Sam and his well-being. However, our church family was a disappointment. They had been so excited for us when we were pregnant but seemed at a loss how to handle the DS news. Looking back, maybe I wasn't strong enough to handle the questions. Maybe I projected my feelings because I felt they pitied our family for having a child with a disability. I expected them to see our baby as a gift from God, not a tragedy. We ended up leaving that small church and chose, instead, to worship with a large congregation where we could be anonymous.

The support never stopped from family and a few special friends who always seemed to have the right words. They were true gifts to us, and I liked how they took the news in stride as if it was no big deal. I needed that!

We also received support from various agencies to help with Sam's development. Living a life of therapy appointments was stressful. I felt pressured to do everything I could to make sure Sam would be the best baby with DS. I joined a parent support group of mothers whose babies also had DS, but instead of being encouraging, I found it stressful. Each mom had her own ideas about the best approach, and many ideas from the support group frustrated me and left me exhausted, so I dropped out.

When Sam was a few months old, God provided a wonderful family of a child born with DS who was a few years older than Sam. They said, "Come eat dinner with us and see that we are an ordinary family." God knew what we needed and they became lifelong friends, a balm to our hearts. We needed to know we could have a normal life despite Sam's differences.

Sam is growing up and well-liked and capable. I think people who see us now think it has been easy. But I want others to know that when a child is born with Down syndrome it is a huge deal with many challenges.

It was hard work to accept God's will for our lives. Sam's "differences" helped us to see life differently and to trust God, and Sam's birth opened my heart to be willing to trust God for other life-changing events. Years later, my husband and I adopted three international children, one of whom has an intellectual disability. We learned to care about God's heart for the least of these and pursued a road less traveled to grow our family. The pre-Sam me wanted smart, successful by the world's standards kids. The post-Sam me wants my children to follow God's will and plan for their lives and for them to fearlessly pursue His call no matter what unexpected events happen.

> "Two roads diverged in a wood, and I—
> I took the one less traveled by,
> And that has made all the difference."
> Robert Frost[18]

God used Sam to grow my faith in Him in a way I cannot explain. I remember that not long after Sam's birth I understood for the first time that God doesn't rescue us from the pit when trials come. Instead, He crawls into the pit with us as a Friend, Teacher, and Comforter. I began to understand Who God is through my challenges. He provided all that I needed to get through those first couple months and years. My trust grew, and I began to worry less about the other shoe dropping and instead trusted that God would be with me to see me through any challenges. Oh, how I love Jesus.

I hope God has used Sam's Down syndrome to bless others. I wish I knew when Sam was born what I know now. I would have said, "Relax, this is going to be hard, but it will be great. Sam is awesome, enjoy the ride." I also hope our life with Sam has encouraged others to see that all individuals with disabilities or differences are created in the image of God just like all able-bodied people. I wouldn't change this life-changing event of having a child born with DS for anything. Sam is fearfully and wonderfully made, created in Christ Jesus to do good works, which God prepared in advance for him to do (Psalm 139:14; Ephesians 2:10).

ENTERING A QUIET HOUSE

-MARILYN-

After Randy's death in Idaho, my daughter Kate and I flew back to Charlotte. Friends met us at the airport, and we hugged and cried.

I stood at the entrance of our home, unable to move, my legs concrete pillars and a boulder residing in my stomach. A tidal wave of emotions flooded my mind as I realized Randy would never come to our home again. Our planned retirement home in a lake community now had a single occupant—me.

The quiet was deafening. It took courage to enter my home. Did I have a choice? The quiet was loud. I entered my home hollow and alone. I placed Randy's suitcase in our closet and closed the door. There was no rush to unpack it.

My daughters and their families arrived at separate times, repeating the scene of somber hugs and tears. My family arranged the funeral plans. While I was present in person, I was in a daze. I sat in my favorite chair and stared off into space, barely hearing the whispered sounds of my family and grandchildren. Was this really happening?

The Christmas tree was up. I would no longer hear my kids call "Dad" or the grandchildren say "Papa." I guess my sons-in-law would take over my husband's job as "master of the grill." I would need to set one less place setting. My use of pronouns would change. There was no more *we*, only *I*.

The mail arrived. As I read the due date on a statement, I realized this was another burden dumped on me. My husband paid the bills. My brain could barely function to microwave a bowl of oatmeal, so my daughter patiently taught me the process of online banking.

I continued to sort the mail and discovered a restaurant gift card Randy ordered as a Christmas gift for our youngest daughter and her soon-to-be fiancé. That afternoon, I gave Doug and Kate the envelope with a note: "Dad ordered this as a gift from both of us to you. When you use it, think of him. Love, Mom." *Love Mom.* Those two words glared at me. It wasn't right, I was supposed to sign "Mom and Dad." When Kate and Doug read the note, their eyes filled with tears. In that moment, Doug silently decided that restaurant would be the spot he would officially propose.

The uncharted territory of entering a quiet house is more than unlocking the door and flicking on the lights. From the outside, the house and door don't change, but behind that door lie memories of the past, changes in conversation, relationships, and activities.

To the discerning eye, changes such as unemployment, relocation, or loss of a career due to illness are obvious. However, silent losses, the ones that go on behind closed doors—the pain of infertility, singleness, a troubled marriage, and loss of friends—roar loudly in broken hearts. Grief and loss are more than a marked event and a date on a calendar. A quiet house speaks.

 What is your quiet house? What does your quiet house mean in terms of conversation, relationships, appearance, and activities?

 "Be still and know I am God."

Psalm 46:10a

RUNNING AGROUND: WILL I ALWAYS FEEL STUCK?

-MARILYN-

"Ladies and gentlemen, this is your captain speaking. This should not have happened, but the ship has run aground."

My husband Randy and I stood against the railing of the cruise ship looking in disbelief as part of the ship floated in the ocean and part rested on the shoreline.

The year was 1970 and my husband and I ushered in the New Year with a Caribbean cruise. We eagerly anticipated the port of Curacao and looked forward to the sights and charm of this former Dutch colony. But our ship had run aground. We watched as the crew tied ropes and tugged. We were immobilized.

In the distance, the distinctive Dutch architecture was inaccessible. Our hope of visiting the oldest synagogue in the Western Hemisphere evaporated.

The captain made a second announcement, "We will be showing the movie *Patton* in the theater during your wait."

Randy raised an eyebrow and said, "Apparently, this problem will not be resolved quickly. *Patton* is nearly three hours long."

Many passengers who waited to shop at this port would return home without their treasures. A dip in the ship's pool replaced scuba diving and snorkeling.

It shouldn't have happened. It wasn't supposed to be like this.

These words echo from a young widow raising two children. She never dreamed her husband would succumb to cancer at age thirty-five.

A man feeding his wife lunch in a nursing home understands the same heartache. "We had retirement plans. Her stroke changed everything."

Carla, a divorced mom, scrambles for money for her ten-year old son's field trip because the child support check is late. Her detailed itinerary of a happy family of five changed when she joined the ranks of single moms. She said, "We ran aground."

Jake, a high school senior, nervously opens an envelope from his first choice college and reads, "We had many applicants and are sorry to inform you . . . " His hopes are dashed.

In 2020, the coronavirus forced non-essential businesses to close. Some of these businesses never reopened. A local mom and pop business is on the brink of failure, eroding the couple's retirement investment and plans for their golden years. In each scenario, plans ran aground.

Like standing on deck and gazing at the unique Dutch architecture in the distance, we compare where we are to where we hope to go. I've heard widows say the second year is worse than the first. And from my experience, I agree. The first year of widowhood is a busy time of adjusting to a quiet house, finding and filing paperwork, and learning new skills. It is changing names on documents and accounts, not to mention the legal nightmare. Widows settle into the reality of finality. At first, people come around and call and pray together. After a year, the calls lessen. I guess others think we've moved on. Beyond that, even when others respond with concern at our life interruption, many do not understand.

April is often asked, "Are you better now?" No, she isn't. She has a chronic illness, and barring a miracle, she will live with it all her life. She functions better some days than others, wears a smile, but she will never return to a healthy body.

Disappointment, heartache, and loss are like a foreign language. Only those who are fluent in the language of a similar loss can understand the internal and spoken dialog.

Eventually, the crew skillfully freed our cruise ship. When we anchored, another surprise met us in the disembarkation line. Since it was New Year's Eve, the shops closed early. My husband and I enjoyed walking the main streets, but those who had shopping in mind were disappointed and were forced to make hasty purchases, settling for less and different than planned. There was no time to take a beach excursion.

When the detour is real and we face a dead end or confusion, it is easy to attach ourselves to false anchors. Unhealthy relationships, shopping, food, alcohol, medications, exercise, are some of the places that give a temporary sense of relief and security. We search for substitutions and try to anchor ourselves at the wrong places. These temporary superficial anchors may stick for a while, but they won't hold us forever. Poor choices may become unsafe, unhealthy, and trap us if we're not careful. Eventually, these false securities will fade or disappoint, and we are in for another loss.

Yet, there is one stable anchor we can turn to. Anchoring our lives firm and secure in Jesus Who sits at the right hand of God will direct and hold me despite living in change. Being anchored to Christ gives me His perspective. Perspective doesn't change the circumstance, but perspective changes me. Having a God-like perspective allows me to understand that God may not remove the difficulty, but He offers His grace and strength to stand firm through the difficulty. "But those who hope in the Lord will renew their strength. They will soar on wings like eagles; they will run and not grow weary, they will walk and not be faint" (Isaiah 40:31). God's perspective reveals His presence in my sorrow, dark thoughts, confusion, and anxiety. His presence gives fullness of complete joy (Psalm 16:11, John 15:11). His presence offers peace. "Peace I leave with you; my peace I give you. I do not give to you as the world gives. Do not let your hearts be troubled and do not be afraid" (John 14:27).

In the disappointment of running aground, when I don't think I can make it through another day, God provides His grace and a firm anchor. "And

God is able to bless you abundantly, so that in all things at all times, having all that you need, you will abound in every good work" (2 Corinthians 9:8).

Consider a time when you felt as if your ship ran aground. Did you sense an anchor? Was it secure or did it eventually fail? Can you identify any false anchors in your life (past or present)? Is there anything you wish you had done differently? Read the Bible verses above. Fill in your personal situations to the principles given and the truths Scripture offers.

"The really happy person is the one who can enjoy the scenery, even when they have to take a detour."

Sir James Hopwood Jeans[19]

"Sometimes God holds you back temporarily until the road is safe and clear to continue. Be thankful for the stall."

Anonymous[20]

MILE MARKER THREE

EXPLORING HOPE IN UNCHARTED TERRITORY

SINGING WITH A BROKEN HEART

How can we sing with a broken heart?

Scorched from the desert sun after walking what seemed like endless miles, the Israelites, God's chosen people, were now slaves, taunted to sing songs that reminded them of their former life at home, a home with freedom, worship, and comfort. How could they sing when their hearts grieved all they'd lost?

"Sing for us!" the Babylonian regimen barked at their new Israelite captives. Exile was bad enough, but now the Babylonians demanded the Israelites sing.

Under their breath, the Israelites grumbled and prayed, "How can we sing the songs of the Lord while in a foreign land?" (Psalm 137:4).

How can *we* sing when suffocated by unwelcome change, loss, and limitations? How dare God and others ask us to sing in a foreign land. Our foreign land may be a new chapter of singleness, a diagnosis, financial challenges, or life-changing news. Regardless, it is unfamiliar, unwanted, and remarkably different from what we planned and now live.

Marilyn's friend Sharon could not sing after the death of her daughter. "I went to church. The words were in my mind, but the melodies didn't make it out of my mouth. I was heartbroken."

Another friend, Claire, related she could not bear to go to church for six months after the death of her husband. "I just couldn't go, surrounded by people and remembering sitting next to each other in a pew. My song was gone."

For some, the inability to sing is figurative. For others, it's literal.

Those of us living in our foreign land masquerade our lack of song. Employers offer three days of bereavement. We return to work, but three days isn't enough time for shock to wear off, much less to begin the grieving process or function normally. But singing? It seems impossible.

What if our experience doesn't come with built-in bereavement days? What then? What if our loss is invisible? How can we operate, much less sing, when the world goes on without acknowledging our earth-shattering news, when the calendar pages turn, holidays appear on schedule, and the days don't remotely resemble our past? Society demands we go on and expects it. We masquerade our struggle and wear a plastic smile to please others or to avoid questions we can't answer.

Singing in a strange land eventually comes, but it doesn't happen easily or overnight. It's often forced. We hear, "You have your life ahead of you." "It's been a year now . . ." Perhaps advice comes, "You'll find another job." "At least your illness is treatable with medication." "You'll have another baby." "It's not the end of the world. There are other colleges to attend." So, we try to remember the words, lip sync a song, or sing off-key. It takes training, discipline, and practice to begin to sing. Scripture tells us to put on "a garment of praise instead of a spirit of despair" (Isaiah 61:3). Usually, it's not the first thing we reach for in the morning; thus, we must intentionally put on the garment of praise to learn to see God for Who He is—sovereign, wise, and yes, loving, in any circumstance. It may be difficult to separate our pain from praise, but the more we shift our focus, the more praise will become our habit and desire.

> "Joy is the serious business of heaven."
> C. S. Lewis[21]

It takes discipline to praise the Lord even when we don't feel His presence or see His hand moving to change our circumstance. But God's Word reminds us He will never leave us nor forsake us (Deuteronomy 31:6). Charles Haddon

Spurgeon, 19th century English pastor, spoke "God is too good to be unkind and He is too wise to be mistaken. And when we cannot trace His hand, we must trust His heart."[22]

Beverly Sills was a gifted American opera singer in the 1960s and 70s. Her coloratura soprano voice received numerous awards and standing ovations. She was also the mother of two special needs children. Her daughter was deaf with multiple sclerosis and her son was severely mentally disabled. In the autobiography, *Bubbles: A Self Portrait*, Sills described her perspective shift about singing. "I needed to sing—desperately. My voice poured out more easily because I was no longer singing for anyone's approval; I was beyond caring about the public's reaction, I just wanted to enjoy myself. I had found a kind of serenity, a new maturity, as a result of my children's problems. I didn't feel better or stronger than anyone else, but it seemed no longer important whether everyone loved me or not—more important now was for me to love them. Feeling that way turns your whole life around; living becomes the act of giving."[23]

No matter the cause of the unexpected detour, let us open the sunroof of our heart, roll the windows down, and throw our hands up in praise to the Lord. By lifting our hearts in praise, we give God what He deserves and invite Him to join us in our journey. Praise doesn't deny, minimize, or remove our loss, but it changes our focus to Who God is, and then it changes us. Look at the following attributes of God and think of how knowing these truths change our perspective. We've only given one Bible reference, but there are other Bible verses that affirm each of these attributes. Taking one a day might be part of your devotional quiet time. What God-confidence and peace can you build if you offered prayers of thanks and praise for these attributes?

Attributes of God

- God is Immutable. He never changes (Malachi 3:6).
- God is Faithful, steadfast and true (Deuteronomy 7:9).

- God is Loving, merciful, and compassionate (Lamentations 3:22–23).
- God is Gracious and desires to save us (Ephesians 1:7).
- God is Good, infinitely kind, and desire to bless us (1 Chronicles 16:34).
- God is Wise and full of perfect wisdom (Romans 11:33).
- God is Just and is right and perfect in all He does (Acts 17:31).
- God is Infinite and without origin (Isaiah 40:28).
- God is Self-sufficient. He has no needs (John 5:26).
- God is Omniscient, all-knowing and has perfect understanding (Psalm 147:5).
- God is Omnipresent, always present everywhere all the time (Colossians 1:17).
- God is Sovereign, Omnipotent, and all powerful (Jeremiah 32:17).
- God is Holy, perfect, divine, and sacred (Revelation 4:8).

Do you find yourself asking, "How in the world do I sing when I am going through such a hard time?" How does the following Scripture help you find your voice?

Ponder Psalm 36:5–7. "Your love, Lord, reaches to the heavens, your faithfulness to the skies. Your righteousness is like the highest mountains, your justice like the great deep. You, Lord, preserve both people and animals. How priceless is your unfailing love, O God! People take refuge in the shadow of your wings."

"If my faith requires a tidy bow or a happy ending then I'm not sure that's faith. Faith is praising Him, when we don't see the ending. When we don't understand what He's up to."

Laura Story[24]

MEET JUDY: PRAYING FOR A PRODIGAL

I often pondered the mystery of children raised in the same home by the same parents taking such diverse journeys as teenagers and adults. But that became our story. The oldest child was disciplined, had a few close friends, was spiritually grounded, and actively involved in our church youth program, a close-knit group with a solid spiritual foundation who remain close friends even today. Our youngest child was outgoing, boisterous, and everyone's friend. His group at church was not close, not consistently involved, and not friends outside the church environment.

We, as his parents, were thrilled that his closest friend was the son of one of our ministers who lived in our neighborhood. He and his wife had sound scriptural practices in their personal lives and in the way they raised their children. When the Lord called them to another church in another city, we were all somewhat heartbroken, especially our son who was losing his closest friend.

Once our son left for college, the accountability to attend church was absent. He became increasingly involved in college athletics and committed himself to excel in his sport. However, he failed to seek or make a connection with a local church body or a community of friends where he could find meaningful spiritual guidance and godly friends. Initially, we were deeply concerned. We prayed fervently for God to draw him back, to place influences in his life that drew him back to the Lord. We were deeply grateful that he stayed closely connected to our family, but we grieved his disconnection with the Lord and with friends who would walk a God-seeking journey.

Even now, we continue to seek and receive the prayer support of extended family and close friends. We also find encouragement in God's Word, which helps us stay grounded on the promises of God. We also find hope in the written works of godly people who have walked the journey. Our personal mentors pray daily for our son and their prayers are medicine to our wounded souls.

Satan is a master at turning our thoughts inward rather than upward. As parents, we have, of course, gone the route of thinking, *what did we do wrong? What could we have done differently?* Satan uses the blame game to attack our hearts and our minds which can often make us overly sensitive to the comments of others. An acquaintance posted on Facebook a few years ago that she believes parents have the key responsibility for protecting their children from becoming a prodigal.

Although I totally understood the premise of her statement, the pain of failure pierced my battered heart. I had to run to the Lord, His Word, His promises, His faithfulness, and His love for comfort. I clearly remember asking the Lord to guard my heart from becoming hard toward that mother whose children all stood firmly in the Lord. While my husband and I did our best, although imperfectly, to raise our children to know the Lord, each child must make a personal, not parental, choice. We had to learn to totally surrender our son to the Lord and pray hard for strength to trust Him to do whatever was necessary to draw our son back to Him.

For anyone else who finds themselves with a prodigal, know this: our hope is in the Lord alone. God alone knows the heart of our prodigals totally and completely. The Lord gave me insight regarding a time in my son's life that profoundly wounded him. When he was thirteen, we had to share with him that his best friend's parents, the ones involved in ministry who moved away when our son was eleven, were getting a divorce. I clearly recall my son's gut-wrenching sobs as he grieved. I still hear his sobbing voice shouting, "I heard them pray. I saw them laugh and love." He reiterated the many memories he had banked in his heart that to him meant their love was real and lasting.

Looking back later when pondering my prodigal, God gave me insight into a spiritual crack in the wall of his heart. The searing pain of loss fractured his view of God. Where was the God who promised to protect those who love Him and serve Him? How could God let this happen? His wounded heart needed attention to heal, but because spiritual wounds aren't visible, we as his parents didn't realize the depth of his wounds. Was there a hardening of His heart toward God? Possibly. Was there an internal wall built around his heart in an effort to self-protect? Only God knows.

While our hearts yearn deeply for our prodigal to return to a vibrant relationship with our heavenly Father, we trust that same heavenly Father to work His will in His timing. That doesn't mean I don't have to speak Scripture over my "mama heart" to remind myself of His faithfulness—I do. There are times I've cried to my Father to help my unbelief, and I have to choose daily to rest in Him, His faithfulness, His perfect love for my son, and His timing. God is using my journey with our prodigal to soften my heart toward others whose children struggle in their spiritual walk. He is also teaching me to rejoice with those whose children have rock solid relationships with the Lord.

TRUSTING GOD WITHOUT A GPS

-MARILYN-

I am directionally challenged. Even around town, I use my GPS or landmarks as crutches to reach familiar destinations. Fifteen years ago, I accompanied my husband on a business trip to Europe. Before we left, I enlisted prayer support for our travel and especially for the times I would be alone. While my husband attended meetings, I was on my own to sightsee and shop. Not only was I unfamiliar with the foreign country, I did not speak the language.

I planned my day using a tourist guide and paper map. I highlighted walking routes downtown and starred places I wanted to see. One goal was a cathedral at the top of a hill. When I arrived, the door was locked. I walked around to the other side and spotted a building next door with a sign on it marked "histoire." Great, I thought. I'll learn about the history of the cathedral. I opened the door only to find a history class in session. The uniformed teenaged girls and the teacher stared at me. Embarrassed, I turned around and kept walking. Sometimes we have to turn around, get our bearings, and step out again.

We may schedule and plan, but we often meet a roadblock. We may misread or misinterpret a situation or find an open door, but when we walk through the door, it's not what we thought. We may be embarrassed by the turn of events in our life, or a new circumstance or life season and its challenges catch us off guard.

When our plans and our new reality collide, we have choices. Where do we go? Which way do we turn? We can stop as if paralyzed, or we can pause to reassess. Perhaps we rest to regain energy and take more time to pray. We keep walking, moving forward despite embarrassment. When I was lost, I prayed. I asked people for help. They tried to help as I asked for assistance in English and my broken French. Sometimes they spoke too fast for me, but they were kind and used gestures to direct me where I should go. Some ignored me. Sometimes, even when we ask for help, others can't give what they don't have or don't want to give.

I realized, at one point, when I saw a familiar building, that I had walked in a circle. I thought I was heading in the right direction, but I wasn't. By then, I was tired, and my feet hurt. I couldn't take a bus because I didn't have the exact change. I knew I would eventually get back to the hotel, so I continued to pray. A cab finally showed up, and I was able to return to the hotel, sore and exhausted. I had walked about eight miles.

When all was said and done, I had to trust God to get me to where I needed to go. During my frustration, I consciously said, "God will get me home. I can trust Him."

When we don't know where we're going, we can trust God to walk with us and get us where we need to be. There may be turns and embarrassing stops, but He will get us to the right place. I left my hotel for the day with insecurity, my map, a tourist guide, plans, and prayer. I think that's the way most of us start our day whether we are at our workplace, at home, or sending our children off to school. We don't know what God has in mind for us on any given day—we may have plans, but we need to be prepared for turns and the unexpected and trust Him.

The next morning, my legs and feet ached. Isn't that the way it is with life-altering hurt—we ache. Our hearts might hurt for our children who are making poor choices, a husband who has lost a job, a diagnosis with an uncertain prognosis, or loneliness that never leaves. When we wake up the next morning, the dilemma, challenge, hurt, or reality of the life interruption is still there, but we can have hope God will get us through, trust in His faithfulness, and know His love never stops. Trusting God and clinging to hope is a daily choice, especially when that choice doesn't come natural to a lot of us.

{
Hope: God will get us through.
Trust: He is faithful.
His love: It never stops.
}

But back to prayer requests for my trip, I prayed for four specific things: safety, wisdom, spiritual lessons to what I experienced, and joy. Yes, we had joy.

In Lausanne I walked in circles with a map I couldn't translate. My aching feet allowed me to stumble upon quiche at a quaint restaurant and later enjoy fondue and chocolate mousse with my husband. I took in sights I had never seen before and learned about a new culture. The same is true for our detours and hard places. If we look hard enough, we can find something of value and something positive in every experience. We can learn and grow.

Later, in my most life-altering season, I remember these profound truths. Each day, if we want to live in hope, we can start our day asking God for direction. We can intentionally ask for wisdom as we make our plans and seek appropriate help as we move along. We can ask God to show us spiritual applications of what is happening in life—what He is teaching us. We can trust Him every step of the way, even in the unfamiliar, rough, uneven places, and when we feel lost. Because even though we ache, He is with us always, and we have security. We may not have chocolate mousse, but we can find joy.

 Do you feel as if you are walking in circles with a map you can't translate? Contemplate what God is teaching you. Have your aching feet stumbled on unexpected treasures?

"Send me your light and your faithful care, let them lead me; let them bring me to your holy mountain, to the place where you dwell. Then I will go to the altar of God, to God, my joy and my delight. I will praise you with the lyre, O God, my God."

Psalm 43:3–4

LOOKING AT LAYERS OF LOSS

-MARILYN-

Three months after my hip surgery, my surgeon cleared me for travel. As I pulled my suitcase on rollers, the casual observer wouldn't know I had physical limitations. My walking had returned to normal, but I was restricted to lifting no more than a gallon of milk. Since I looked able-bodied, the airline employee didn't see my need for assistance and motioned for me to lift my suitcase on the scale. When Randy was alive, he would have lifted the luggage. Now, I stood there incredulous, wondering what to do. The airline employee said she wasn't allowed to lift my suitcase on to the scale. A kind gentleman overheard the conversation and offered to help. At that moment, the airline employee "broke the rules" and took my suitcase.

My limitations presented a picture of secondary losses. Losses are often obvious measurable experiences or changes. Dependence on a cane or wheelchair is visible. A "For Sale" sign in the yard announces a need to downsize because of job loss. An infertile couple remains a couple after years of marriage. A gaunt frame and clumps of missing hair are the observable signs of cancer, chemotherapy, or radiation. All are visible primary losses.

During our pandemic, we experienced a threat to our health. For some, their primary loss was of health or a loved one. Others felt boxed in by the daily lack of freedom and face-to-face communication due to government stay-at-home orders.

Our secondary losses of social and physical distancing led to isolation—no hugs from grandchildren or friends gathering around the dining room table. Employees were furloughed and businesses shuttered. Vacation plans evaporated or were tentative at best. This unplanned and unpredicted medical and financial crisis was front and center in the news and on social media. Some become depressed, and mental health suffers; the unknown is scary. Tensions rose in homes. Reports indicate domestic abuse and prescriptions for anxiety meds increased. Although schools continued via bussing to provide two meals a day to children, some children still did not eat well. The coronavirus presented a primary loss of real or threatened health with secondary tentacles affecting every aspect of life.

Loss, like baggage in the overhead bin, is never far from reach. A divorced mom must share her children for holidays. Christmas, without seeing her children wake up with wide eyes and smiles at gifts under the tree, feels empty and unnatural. The secondary heartbreak of missing her children on a special holiday intensifies the pain of the primary loss of a marriage and family.

Moving to a new state involves more than selling and buying a house and unpacking boxes. Secondary losses of rooted, trustworthy friendships cause us to lament over friends and the life we left behind. This becomes apparent when an invitation to lunch in a new town reveals little connection with current residents. Although a group of women graciously invited you, eventually, their conversation turns to shared historical experiences you know nothing about. You return home with the ache of loss and desired connection.

> Loss, like baggage in the overhead bin, is never far from reach.

Unfulfilled dreams are among future secondary losses. Parents, whose child died at age eight, will experience the loss of unfulfilled dreams ten years later when neighbors in their child's class celebrate high school graduation. The mom who had a stillborn baby observes friends' laughter over first steps and the first day of school for their children who would be the same age. Their hearts hurt for the unfulfilled dream, for what could have been.

Losses have layers, and over time they take on different shape. When my husband died, I was on my own to unravel home and auto repairs. I wondered, what do I do now? Who can I call? Do I Google to find the answer? Maybe YouTube will lead me through a repair, so at least I can know what I'm looking for and ask an intelligent question. I found myself asking a

> "For our light and momentary troubles are achieving for us an eternal glory that far outweighs them all."
> 2 Corinthians 4:17

friend, "How did you manage this? Do you have advice for me? Does the hurt and 'one more thing' ever stop?"

Some secondary losses seem oversized and too heavy to bear. They're bulky and don't fit in the overhead bin. Some are tackled once; others reoccur. Initially, we may feel helpless, but we are not hopeless. In humility I had to make needs known and accept help when I cringed at doing so. By joining my heart with God's, participating in a grief support group, and knowing others face similar challenges, I found hope. Now years later, I offer encouragement to others in similar needs. My faith has held on to hope.

Yes, secondary losses continue. We don't deny them, but we can adjust and can get through them. We have hope because God promises, "Never will I leave you; never will I forsake you" (Hebrews 13:5b). His grace will meet our need. "Even to your old age and gray hairs I am he, I am he who will sustain you" (Isaiah 46:4a). He keeps His promises and never lets go.

Have you identified secondary losses? Pray and surrender them to God. Ask for His strength and guidance in this uncharted territory, knowing there will be future secondary losses.

"When it feels like hope can't be found, when we don't even know how we're going to put one foot in front of the other, Scripture teaches us that's when grace abounds."
Laura Story[25]

STAYING IN ALIGNMENT: TRIGGERS AND TRUST

~APRIL~

Our family drove past a woman approximately my age jogging through the neighborhood. A single tear trailed down my cheek. Transfixed, I watched her ponytail sway with each measured stride. I pondered her music playlist and envied her ability to run.

My daughter noticed me wiping away the tear. "Mom?"

"I used to run. I miss running. I miss being active and . . . " The words trailed off.

I inhaled deeply, attempting to hold back tears, control my breathing, and steady my thoughts. My attempt failed as a sorrowful wail surged from the depths. The sight of this woman running scraped the bottom of my soul and dredged up shards of grief, pieces of me before I became ill. The woman running triggered a memory, transporting me in time to when I too ran through the neighborhood.

Triggers come out of nowhere and often at a most inconvenient time. Triggers do not care if you are meeting with a potential business client who wears the same cologne as your late husband, or if you walk into an antique store and recognize your late grandmother's embroidered linens. Triggers taunt and evoke an emotional flashflood. We often stuff our response. Who wants to be around a grumpy person or a person who breaks into sobs? Early in grief, Marilyn knew she would feel like a fifth wheel at a dinner party— the odd seat at the table of seven—and declined the invitation. Even now, she is selective in knowing her comfort level with a group of couples.

86

Triggers are unavoidable. As I wrote in "Silencing the Holiday Road Rage," one year, I did not want to celebrate Thanksgiving or Christmas. I confess, I wanted to jump from October to January and be over the holiday hoopla. Holidays and special days can trigger our thoughts of a loved one or a time *before* our unwanted event. I classify my life as before I was sick and now. Widows and parents, who have lost a child, do the same—holidays before loss and now. Most will even say they'd like to fast-forward November to January. Even in marriage, my husband and I joke about the extra money and spontaneity of our life BC (before children).

Although I have accepted my illness, unsuspecting waves of grief and despair can knock me down. I understand from others that triggers last a lifetime. Just because association and memories provoke tears or sadness, though, doesn't mean I'm stuck in grief. It means the memories I hold represent significant moments in my life. They helped shape me and wrote a meaningful chapter of my life. Triggers will come, but they won't always feel as heavy. I may cry, linger for a bit, and reflect on its significance, but then I move forward, leaning on God's promises.

When wrestling with triggered memories, I reflect on the words of David in Psalm 13. "How long must I wrestle with my thoughts and day after day have sorrow in my heart? How long will the enemy triumph over me? But I trust in your unfailing love; my heart rejoices in your salvation. I will sing the Lord's praise, for he has been good to me" (Psalm 13:2, 5–6).

 Have you learned to recognize your triggers? How have you learned to cope with them? Do you feel trapped by memories?

 "God gave us memory so we might have roses in December."

J. M. Barrie[26]

DISCOVERING UNEXPECTED FRIENDSHIPS

-APRIL-

I didn't know I'd meet my next best friend on October 18, 2015.

My daughter Rachel invited two friends home for a sleepover. As with most fifth-grade girls, they giggled, painted their nails, and watched movies late into the night. On Saturday afternoon, my husband and I had made plans to take our family and the girls to the local pumpkin patch where we arranged for the other parents to pick up the girls.

The girls skipped through the corn maze, danced in fields of sunflowers, and raced each other through the pumpkin patch. I watched in awe and wonder as tears invisible behind my sunglasses had escaped to my cheeks. Despite the girls' laughter, sorrow filled my heart. In less than a year, seven friends had moved away. One friend moved across the state of Virginia, while others moved to Texas, Florida, Illinois, Germany, and two moved to Tennessee. True meaningful friendships are hard to find. I was heartbroken for the loss of so many within a short period.

Turning my attention back to my daughter and her friends; I recall one of the girls had been friends with my daughter since preschool, while the other girl, Jenna, was new to the school.

Jenna saw me wiping away tears and asked, "Mrs. White, are you okay?"

"I will be, Jenna. I'm just a little sad today."

In ten-year old innocence, she asked, "But it's a beautiful day, why are you sad?"

Sighing, not knowing how much to share with a ten-year-old, I decided to share the truth. "To be honest, I'm sad because several of my good friends have moved away in the past few months. I miss my friends."

Like Pollyanna, she singsongs a solution, "We're new here and my mom doesn't have a lot of friends. You and my mom can be friends."

I didn't know much about Jenna and her family, other than the mom was a stay-at-home mom and their nanny drove her luxury model SUV. Our vehicles had over one hundred thousand miles. I was nervous to meet this mother. I didn't run in the same socio-economic groups as people with a nanny or a luxury vehicle.

Meg, Jenna's mother, arrived at the pumpkin patch looking like an L. L. Bean model in jeans and a fleece vest. "One more thing not in common," I thought.

Jenna bounced to greet her mom and said, "Mommy, Mrs. White is sad because several of her friends have moved away. But I told her that you two could be friends."

To my surprise, our personalities meshed, and we became instant friends. Meg and I began spending more time together, often meeting in the school carpool line early to talk. Learning the reason why Meg stays at home and has a nanny demolished my preconceived impression. For over twenty years, Meg has dealt with reoccurring brain tumors, radiation, and chemotherapy.

Soon after our meeting in October 2015, my own health began a downward spiral and Meg's cancer returned with vengeance. *But God* (all good things come after those two words) knew this and He prepared a new friendship for us to be "mutually encouraged by each other's faith" (Romans 1:12). Our friendship grew richer with each passing year.

Since the beginning of this manuscript, my beloved Meg passed. She was the one friend I felt understood me the most. There are times I reach for my phone to text her. I think about meeting for our routine Starbucks and realize she's not here. She was my Irish friend who died on St. Patrick's Day. When

I see a shamrock, advertisements, or silly St. Patty's day garb, I think of Meg. There is still a piece of me that feels empty and I imagine there always will.

One of my favorite quotes on friendship is by Oprah Winfrey: "Lots of people want to ride with you in the limo, but what you want is someone who will take the bus with you when the limo breaks down." Storms and suffering test the durability of friendships. Not all friendships we have at the beginning of our journey will remain at the end. Not all friendships are water resistant or fireproof. God brings us into deep waters of pain and suffering with Him so we can learn to trust Him.

Suffering purges friendships. It is a hard reality to acknowledge, but it is true. Not all friendship purging is malicious. Some friends don't handle our critical change. They don't know what to say or do. So, instead of saying the wrong thing, they say nothing. Their initial lack of recognition of our life-changing event subtly turns into lack of eye contact and unreturned calls or messages. Over time, our once close friends avoid us all together. They sit somewhere else in church, avoid us in the carpool line, or don't return emails or phone calls.

Guilt begins to set in for them because so much time has lapsed without communication or without mention of our situation. I have shared this scenario with many people and the one thing I want others to know is this: It is never too late to reach out to a friend going through a difficult time. There are no magic words, but an honest and sincere apology for not reaching out when it mattered the most is a great way to start. Acknowledging your personal discomfort and admitting you didn't know what to say as the reason for your lack of communication, will often be met with understanding appreciation.

The bonds of friendship forged during suffering can withstand the heat of new battles. God sets aside the purest friendships for great trials and suffering. Not only did God present me with Meg's friendship, but since that time, other friendships have ripened in connection, spiritual maturity, and spiritual growth. These friendships help hold me up in prayer when I feel particularly weary from illness, raising teens, and secondary losses.

 Write the names of lost friendships. Now, write the names of new friends who have entered your life in this new season. How has your circumstance altered your approach to friendships?

 "Lots of people want to ride with you in the limo, but what you want is someone who will take the bus with you when the limo breaks down."

Oprah Winfrey[27]

MEET DOROTHY: TAKING BACK HER HEALTH

I struggled with respiratory allergies since my early thirties. After countless appointments and tests, doctors confirmed a diagnosis of severe allergies to mold. You would think that, after identifying the problem, my life would get easier, but the years of damage to my body were irreversible.

The work involved in protecting myself from mold is difficult. My doctor recommended my husband and I move, not merely relocate to another home, but leave all furniture and contents. That wasn't a realistic option for us, so we opted to modify our home. One year and $40,000 later, we continue with major projects to maintain a mold-free home, and we spend $6,000 annually to maintain the air quality in our home.

My illness is simple yet complex. Although many people have allergies, mine are extreme. Allergens such as mold, perfumes, or contaminants can cause a severe allergic flare. I then need isolation, either to avoid contaminated areas or other people. When I have an attack, it can take a day to recover.

Because I do not look sick and I can perform normal life functions, people are unaware of my condition. People don't understand how life altering it is. Along with a chronic illness comes emotional strain since there seems to be no end in sight. In addition to mold, I continue to deal with anxiety and depression.

Whenever one has a life-altering health experience, there is stress and uncertainty. My focus and outlook rest on knowing God uses all circumstances in our lives to teach us. I encourage others to seek God and ask what He wants us to learn through the circumstance. Stay in tune with God and express anger, disappointments, and discouragement. He knows our thoughts and emotions. Seek God to understand how He is using this hardship to shape us. We must be willing to walk the path of suffering. Remember we are a work in progress. Don't give up seeking a diagnosis and treatment. Continue searching for answers even if you feel there is no hope. There was a time I stopped searching for an answer because I didn't think it existed. I lost time and this hurt me in the end.

Knowing God loves me and has a plan for me is the cornerstone of my life. My faith allows me to persevere and trust God. I have difficult days and I don't always have the faith I should, but I cannot imagine going through this without believing in God and His purposes for me.

When I was diagnosed, my doctors wanted me to stay in my "safe" environment as much as possible. My husband worked long hours, and we had no children at home. I felt alone and isolated. I could have stayed in my depression and misery and escaped through watching TV, but I chose to pray and read His Word and see what God had in mind for me. During those two years, He prepared my heart for my ministry. Since then, God has given me opportunities to share my story, the lessons He has taught me, and talk with people who have chronic illnesses.

You can find more about Dorothy Deming's story in the resources.

WE NEVER WALK ALONE

Although we miss our lake view, we love the convenience of suburban life. After living in a rural community for eighteen years, the thrill of Christmas morning excitement pulsed through our veins over curbside trash pickup, pizza delivery, and high-speed internet. Situated on the outskirts of our new neighborhood, the middle and high school buildings are a twenty-minute walk from our home. I told the kids, if they missed the bus, they'd walk to school. When my daughter missed the bus on picture day, I relented and offered to drive her to school. Visibly relieved, she sighed and her shoulders relaxed. As I pulled out of the driveway, my daughter cranked up the newest pop music boy band. Rachel anxiously chatted about the bus traffic, being late to school, and possibly sent to the principal's office.

I sipped the dark brew of liquid mercy and hid my smug smile. She did not know I planned a different route. She expected me to drop her off at the front of school. However, departing that carpool line is a thirty-minute hassle. Instead, I pulled the car over to a walking trail behind the school.

Rachel turned in her seat. "Hey, there's Marcus."

"Oh good, you know him?"

"Yeah."

I turned back to Rachel and displayed my confident you're-not-going-to-like-what-I'm-about-to-say parental grin. "Good. Now you don't have to walk alone."

"What? You're not driving me to school?" she questioned.

"This is the trail behind the school. Go ahead, get out, and walk with Marcus."

She was stunned. I drove her to school as promised, but I didn't deliver her via the anticipated route. Instead, she would walk the short trail connecting our neighborhood to the school, bypassing the traffic. But she would not walk alone.

At some point, we all find ourselves walking an unexpected path. We can rest in the hope we never walk alone. When the path we planned shuts down, God provides another way. Often, we map life goals in a linear and logical plan, but God may provide a difficult path.

When I think back over my unanticipated journey of illness, job loss, move, and betrayal of friends, I can point to precise moments along the path when God provided a friend when I needed one the most. Sometimes the companions who linked arms with me were cherished old friends. Other times, they were new friends, sent by divine appointment, who understood my new struggle of suffering.

When I experience dark moments, when brokenness overwhelms me, I allow myself to cry. These are the days when my social media activity and text messages remain silent. I cry for myself and for God's help. God is the lifter of my head (Psalm 3:3). His Word reminds me He will never leave us nor forsake me (Deuteronomy 31:6).

As a sojourner on an unexpected path, think about a time when God provided a way. Write names of friendships given by divine appointment or in a critical season of life. Or write about the times when you were physically alone, but God's presence was your Friend. Regardless of where you are, rest assured, you will never walk alone.

"Sometimes God will interrupt your progress in order to get your attention. Sometimes he does that as an act of grace because he sees you expending effort in the wrong direction. What you are calling progress is actually paralysis from heaven's perspective."

Steven Furtick[28]

NEW JOURNEY: NEW VEHICLE

"I'm a big girl now," I joked with my husband when I purchased my first used car at the age of twenty-three. Fast-forward five years, I was weeks away from being a mother and needed a vehicle to accommodate a car seat and my growing belly. With a few signatures, I traded in a sporty red Mazda MX-6 for a sensible Volkswagen Passat. This was another rite of passage as I now drove a mom-mobile.

Five years after that, I paid off my student loan debt. I rewarded myself by selling the VW Passat and purchasing a gently used two-door red convertible. I loved leaving work and driving home with the top down. The wind whipped my hair back, and I felt such a sense of freedom. As my children grew taller, however, so did their gear. Book bags, gym bags, lunch boxes, and soccer or softball bags could no longer fit in my car. My little red convertible needed to go.

Despite my love for the freedom, I desired space more. In 2014, I traded my convertible for a one-year-old Volkswagen Passat diesel. Little did I know how much I would later need this to accommodate a currently dormant illness. I purchased the one-year-old VW diesel fully equipped with the latest gadgets and gizmos. How had I lived this long without heated seats and lumbar support? The spacious back seats allowed me to recline the passenger seat during the three-hour drives (one way) to Duke for treatment. Summer or winter, I use the heated seats every day. The warmth helps ease my chronic muscle pain. God is in the details. Even though I thought I was the one making the car changes; God was placing these thoughts in my mind to prepare the way for a future need.

My gently used VW diesel was part of the VW scandal where the automaker falsified the diesel emissions to the EPA. Because of the court settlement, I had the car fixed and VW awarded me a lump sum of money. I used the money to pay off my car. Again, God is in the details. Even before I knew my illness would render me unable to work, God was taking care of my financial needs.

God is in the details of life. Even the most inconsequential area, areas you don't even know exist (like my illness dormant for forty years), God is at work. He has gone ahead of us, preparing in ways unknown to us. He has compassion for us and loves us. Trust Him in the details. Not one detail escapes Him. He knows everything.

-MARILYN-

"No woman your age should be in a car with over 100,000 miles," Ann's son advised her. Ann, a widowed friend of mine, shared this story with me over dinner. My antennae buzzed. My vehicle approached nearly 140,000 miles. I had been thinking about trading it, and our discussion confirmed my need to make another major decision, and with it, a big change. As women alone, we agreed we needed safe and reliable vehicles.

I did my research, sought counsel, and prayed for wisdom to make the right decision. My late husband had always investigated our vehicle choices. In the past, I test drove the vehicles he narrowed down, and we made decisions together, but he had done all the legwork. This was a new, solo path. Another road on unwanted and uncharted territory.

I felt comfortable with my decision until I began emptying my Honda Pilot and found an auto maintenance book with my husband's signature. Although I'd driven this car for four and half years now, this was my husband's vehicle. It was more than a mode of transportation, but a collection of memories on wheels—memories of driving to church together every Sunday, visiting family in PA, and moving one daughter from PA to NC. A glance in the back seat triggered memories of our family occupying two rows of seats to head to a restaurant or on vacations. Miles of memories were logged in the odometer and in my heart.

Selling my husband's car was another secondary loss. Before I left to get my new vehicle, I stood at my kitchen sink and looked up at a prayer card on my windowsill. There it was, Psalm 37:3-5, "Trust in the Lord and do good; dwell in the land and enjoy safe pasture. Take delight in the Lord, and he will give you the desires of your heart. Commit your way to the Lord; trust in him and he will do this."

Between that verse, my conversation with my friend, and the encouragement from family telling me, "Dad would have traded this in three years ago," I felt confident I was following the right path.

I dropped off my vehicle, picked up the new one, and drove slowly past my black Honda Pilot, catching one final look. As I drove off the dealership lot, I left behind another attachment to my husband. I still have the memories and now a new car smell, but most of all, I have the commitment to trust God and to know He will help me today and in whatever follows.

Ambiguity shrouds most decisions. When we face critical decisions, we can move forward with confidence in God if we pray, look at Biblical principles, and receive wise counsel from friends.

 Take a few minutes to look back. Have you replaced anything in your new journey? Was it voluntary or were you forced to give it up? Have you recognized God's work in life?

 "Trust in the Lord and do good; dwell in the land and enjoy safe pasture. Take delight in the Lord, and he will give you the desires of your heart. Commit your way to the Lord; trust in him and he will do this."

Psalm 37:3-5

"Getting over a painful experience is much like crossing monkey bars. You have to let go at some point in order to move forward."[29]

MILE MARKER FOUR

SHIFTING PERSPECTIVE TOWARD HOPE

-APRIL-

In 2016, I walked away from work for extensive medical testing, eager for God to "name it, claim it, so I could move on." But my painful and periodic debilitating symptoms continued without a diagnosis. Until that point, I never realized the importance of naming an illness. My painful symptoms continued because the doctors needed to know what condition I had before initiating treatment. Without a name, my treatment was delayed.

Confusion and agony invaded my thoughts. The pharmacist in me urged the patient in me to remain calm. I'd say to myself, *some illnesses take extra time to diagnose. The doctors need to rule out a variety of other causes.* However, the patient in me was running out of patience.

New challenges accompanied each step into the unwelcomed land of chronic illness. As I waited for a medical name for my bizarre symptoms, my curious thoughts zigzagged from Lyme's Disease to Multiple Sclerosis to Lupus to Myasthenia Gravis and any other disease with similar symptoms. At times, the anxiety caused by waiting simmered like a whistling teakettle. I desperately begged God to expedite the waiting process so a doctor could, "name it," we'd "claim it," and I could "move on." Naming and confirming my illness with a second opinion at Duke Medical Center took thirteen agonizing months: Hypokalemic Periodic Paralysis.

Silly me. I thought once I had a name for my condition, the "claim it" part of medication or treatment would be easy so I could move on. I was unprepared for the emotional upheaval in my soul that tagged along when I heard the words, "There is no cure." *No cure.* Please don't gloss over those two words. Even as I write, my eyes well up with tears and I pray for each person who will read these words—for each person who heard them, too.

Many face chronic situations that are not health related and without a cure: a broken marriage, loss of a child, loss of a loved one, infertility, or emotional turmoil from abuse. For us, the "claim it and move on" area is the hardest. Many have wreckage in our past we need to "name" and release into the capable hands of God. This takes time and may require the aid of a trained counselor, prayer, work, and choices. The spiritual implications of names were not lost on me during my waiting season. While I waited, I focused on the names of God and the names God gives His children. I also reminded myself God's promises never fail. Using multicolored pens, I highlighted the passages of Scripture that reference waiting on God. I wrote key verses and names on index cards and sticky notes and posted them throughout the house. Here is a sampling of my journal entries during this time:

- "We have this hope as an anchor for the soul, firm and secure" (Hebrews 6:19a).
- God is our Jehovah-jireh: The God Who Provides. "God himself will provide" (Genesis 22:8a).
- "I keep my eyes always on the Lord. With him at my right hand, I will not be shaken" (Psalm 16:8).
- "Be still, and know that I am God" (Psalm 46:10a).
- "If we are faithless, he remains faithful, for he cannot disown himself" (2 Timothy 2:13).
- "The one who calls you is faithful, and he will do it" (1 Thessalonians 5:24).
- "Wait for the Lord; be strong and take heart and wait for the Lord" (Psalm 27:14).

I don't want to convey that I had immediate acceptance or peace, but I did know where to begin—the truth of God's Word. But while I'm sharing entries from my prayer journal, let me also share one of my many less-than-perfect moments. This story took place within the first six weeks of my leave of absence. What I didn't know at the time was that I would never return to work as a pharmacist. My pain was raw, and I reacted in anger. From my journal:

My friend Meg called to check on me. Battling a reoccurring brain tumor for the past twenty years, Meg understood the complexities and range of emotions that accompany illness. She inquired about my test results, future appointments, and overall next step. I filled her in on every detail, giving her the long story long because I knew she truly cared and understood.

Restless and exasperated, I finally said, "I'm halfway through my paid short-term disability. God has six more weeks to figure out what's wrong with me so I can 'name it, claim it, and move on.'"

I regretted the words as soon as they flew out of my mouth. Leaning against the kitchen counter, I whispered, "Hold on Meg." With the call still connected, I dropped my hand holding the phone and prayed aloud:

"Lord, please forgive me. Forgive me for putting a time limit on You. Lord, You are Sovereign above all. You don't need to figure out what is wrong with me because You already know. You knit me together in my mother's womb. Nothing about my being escapes Your notice. Lord, I trust in You. Amen."

I lifted the phone back up. "Meg, did you hear that?"

"Yeah, I did. You've been healthy and in control for so long that I think it is common to feel this way at first. But God knows. He sees your needs and knows every detail. He's never going to leave you nor forsake you."

We continued talking and she prayed with me. (Here I am thinking that I should be the one encouraging her, but she is the one who is encouraging me.) I appreciated her friendship. Many times, especially at the beginning of my illness, I didn't know how to process my own thoughts much less articulate those thoughts to others. But Meg understood because she'd been walking on the path of illness for years. She came alongside me at the right time to infuse hope.

Later, I would name and claim this day with Meg's phone call and prayer, my selfish words, and my surrender as a marker for my life. On this day, I drove a spiritual stake in the ground and took my first step of complete surrender.

In 2016, I reacted with anger, now with the hindsight of twenty-twenty vision, I respond with acceptance. I see God's hand guiding my illness, my family, and every single detail. No detail was too small for God to handle, including the day I prayed for God to provide the money for genetic testing. Hours later a woman from Bible study visited me and said she felt God prompting her to give to me. She handed me a check for one thousand dollars. My friends did not know about the cost of the genetic testing. But God knew. He prompted this woman to generously give the exact amount I had prayed for earlier that morning.

Storyteller and missionary Otto Koning, shares in his *Pineapple Story* series, "God takes good care of His property."[30] I now understand this truth for myself. Prior to my illness, I believed in God and I believed in His sovereignty. However, my husband had a good job, and I had a lucrative profession. If we wanted something, we bought it. We budgeted for vacations, and if necessary, we worked extra hours. We were, like many Americans, reaping the benefits of hard work. Independence and self-sufficiency are qualities we desire to instill in our children for a proper launch into adulthood; however, independence and self-reliance are not the qualities God desires in His children. When we rely on ourselves and not on God as our Source, we are, as Otto Koning states, "Leaving God unemployed."[31]

God revealed the name of my chronic illness and along with it the words, "No cure." My "claim it" was to embrace His choices and work in my life to fulfill His purposes for me. The moving on? I moved the pharmacist lab coat to the back of the closet because God has chosen a new path for me. I trust His promises and grab for His grace for every step.

God's shoulders are big enough to handle our anger and pain. It's okay to tell Him we're angry about this circumstance.

Anger is one part of the grief cycle. What aspect of your circumstance were you most angry about? How does "name it, claim it, and move forward" relate to your life?

"God's shoulders are big enough to handle our anger and pain."

April White

WHO TOLD YOU THAT? DEBUNKING LIES AND RECALCULATING THOUGHTS

~APRIL~

"Who do you think you are writing a book? Why would anybody listen to you?" Often doubts of my new purpose and role jump and hide like a prairie dog. These negative thoughts weasel in and catch me off guard. I squeeze my eyes shut and mentally wallop the weasels back in their hole, like the children's whack-a-mole game; however, these rude rodent thoughts are too quick and pervasive for me.

I once heard someone refer to negative thoughts, as "stinkin' thinkin'." I love this phrase and I use it all the time. With my southern accent, the phrase melts together like butter on a biscuit. We are not immune to stinkin' thinkin', those pesky thoughts that pop in at random times like the carpool line and whisper, "You're not a cool mom." or "She's had five children and no muffin top, what's wrong with you?" Currently, my husband and I are wrestling with God (and rattling the gates of heaven in prayer) over our prodigal child. We both often hear these thoughts, "You're a failure as a parent. If you had raised your child differently, you wouldn't be in this dilemma."

Please note I am not referring to deep depression or suicidal ideations. I've been there before with postpartum depression and bad notions that accompanied my illness. In the first case, I saturated my mind in God's Word, chiefly Psalms and Isaiah. His Word alone lifted me from the pit of postpartum depression. My second battle with depression developed with my chronic illness. This time, depression invited suicidal ideas to tag along. I did not keep these thoughts in the dark. I told my husband and my neurologist. I also told my counselor who was helping me handle my grief over the changes of life. Over time, I felt less hollow. God, counseling, medication, and a supportive family aided in my recovery. Joy returned, little by little.

When worrisome thoughts and stinkin' thinkin' flood my mind, I ask myself two questions: *Where did this come from? Who told you that?* Recalling Paul's letter to the church at Corinth, he reminds the early believers to "take captive every thought to Christ" (2 Corinthians 10:5). Unlike Paul's readers, we have the luxury of holding the entire cannon of God's Word in one book, the Bible.

God's Word is our weapon to rebuke the stinkin' thinkin' thoughts of the enemy. In Ephesians 6:17, Paul refers to God's Word as the "sword of the Spirit" as part of the armor of God. The Word of Truth can extinguish the enemy's schemes. Here is a list of truth statements we can claim when fighting doubt, negative thoughts, or our true purpose.

I am:

- Unstoppable—Nothing formed against me shall prevail (Isaiah 54:17).
- Fearfully and wonderfully made (Psalm 139:14).
- Sustained and strengthened day-by-day though my sword is marred and my shield is dented (Psalm 89:21).
- Guided by God (Isaiah 30:21).
- Comforted by God (Psalm 119:48–52).
- Unable to hide from His presence (Psalms 139:7–12).
- I am His (Isaiah 43:1).

Need more hope? Additional statements of truth are located in the resource section.

The enemy is a master deceiver and the father of lies (John 8:44). His greatest desire is for us to doubt Who God is and Who He says He is and for us to doubt God's Word, the Bible. The enemy wants us to believe the lies and negative thoughts. When negative thoughts arise, we should ask, "Who told you that?" If it does not agree with God's Word, then it isn't true. Friend, if you walk with the Lord, your joy will return little by little.

What negative thoughts or doubt do you wrestle with most often? Who told you that? Is there anything in your mind that you need to take captive to turn it over to Christ? Which of these "I am" proclamations resonated with you the most? Consider writing a prayer on an index card to help you battle the next round of stinkin' thinkin'.

"Don't let the enemy run away with your mind."

Robert Morris, Pastor of Gateway church[32]

FRIENDSHIP IN CHANGING SEASONS

-MARILYN-

My husband swam in a sea of giggles as our three girls chatted about their first day of school. The incessant dinner chatter was music to our ears. They vied for time to talk about their teachers and friends. Our oldest, a high school freshman, lamented that she and her best friend didn't have the same schedule. The girls remarked how much the boys grew over summer break. My husband and I encouraged our youngest to reach out to welcome new classmates and invite them to play at recess. Then, the nonstop conversation turned to me. Susan asked if I had seen Mrs. Lawson lately. During the summer, our families enjoyed our pool time together nearly every day.

"No, I haven't," I answered, a little surprised by her inquiry.

"Oh, I figured since you always sat at the pool together, you might talk on the phone or something."

"Well, the Lawsons go to a different school, so no, I haven't seen her."

Then in wisdom that surpassed her years, Susan, almost reflectively, said, "Oh. Mrs. Lawson is a circumstantial friend."

Frankly, I hadn't heard relationships categorized that way, but yes, our friendship was based on circumstances, namely time at the pool. It's not that we didn't like each other. We did. We talked for hours while the kids swam, but once pool season ended, we went separate ways.

We also can have seasonal friends, those who show up in a specific season of our life. Mothers experience this with other mothers of our children's classmates.

When children grow up or change schools or grade levels, their parents' friendships change, too. The same is true for our co-workers. We might be friends in the workplace, go to lunch together, and bond over a project, but the friendship changes when we resign, retire, or change jobs. When I lived in a small town for five years, our neighborhood was a tight group of friends, but that changed when I moved. Relocation to a new community and finding a church brings opportunities for making new friends or sometimes being friendless for a while.

The popularity of social media has changed the definition of "friend." We accept friend requests on Facebook from people we don't know well. They may be a mutual friend or a classmate from high school whose photo we don't recognize. If you look at someone's profile, you might see hundreds of friends. Some may be acquaintances, professional contacts, or members of an organization.

Friends, by definition, are people with whom you share an affection and life connection. Friends support and encourage one another and often share confidences and trust. Unlike social networking "friends," contacts, and followers, we know our real friends well.

{ Disappointment can be an opportunity in disguise. }

One aspect of friendship often not considered, is a change in friendships as an outcome of a loss. Though a widow feels uncomfortable in a group of couples, there can be more to changes in friendships than being a single in a Noah's Ark couple's world.

Early on, two friends told me not to take offense when (not if) some married women begin to distance themselves from me. It caught me by surprise, and I thought, "I don't think so." I was even more surprised when it became reality.

No, they didn't "break up" with me like a teenager and her boyfriend in high school. It was subtle; the phone calls and emails stopped, a suggestion to get together was postponed or avoided. Someone told me, "It's because they see you and think that they could be a widow. When they don't see you, it's out of sight, out of mind." Another went so far as to speculate that these women were threatened and thought I might take their husband. (I laughed at that idea; surely that wasn't the case with my friends.) I admit their loss of contact and friendship was a painful part of my grief. It was loss on top of loss. They had shared life with us as a couple, knew my husband, and could recall memories that would make me smile, but that vanished when they did. It was also an unnecessary assault imposed by others at a heartbreaking time.

Friendships change in loss and hard times. Some friends choose to step away or terminate friendship rather than provide encouragement. Perhaps they don't know how to respond. As time goes by, they recognize they never stepped in and said anything, and feeling guilty, they choose to stay away. But we do not have to impose isolation on ourselves. We can look for new opportunities, seek new friendships, and encourage others.

Disappointment can be an opportunity in disguise. Loss of friendships can morph into unusual gain. Eventually, I met new friends who understood my new season.

When I went to Grief Share, the facilitator offered a prayer for God to fill our empty spaces. One of those answers came in the support I had from neighbors and women at church in the early months of grief. Later, I met many widows when I relocated. We understood each other, supported new widows, shared meals and Bible studies, and traveled and attended events together. We linked arms in understanding and camaraderie. God answered that prayer for empty spaces with new friends and more of Him.

How have friendship disappointments led you to new opportunities? How have you reached out to make new friends? What have new friendships meant to you? What have you learned about being a friend?

"The greatest healing therapy is friendship and love."

Hubert H. Humphrey[33]

SILENCING HOLIDAY ROAD RAGE

~APRIL~

I caught my inner two-year-old throwing a temper tantrum. She screamed, "I don't want this stupid illness! I don't want to move! I want to go back to work!" My inner two-year-old huffed and stomped. Pictures rattled against the walls as I slammed the bedroom door for some alone time.

I'd like to admit I handled the news of my illness with grace and dignity. In reality, especially in the early months on my illness, I behaved like a spoiled rotten two-year-old overdue for a nap. No matter how much I clomped through the house, stared off into space, or cried, it would not change my situation.

As Thanksgiving approached, I admitted to my husband that I wanted to skip the holidays and go straight to January. My heart was too heavy with the burden of the unknowns. I hadn't sorted out my feelings of what was happening in my life. Naturally, I did not want to have a conversation with distant family members who would ask me the same taxing questions I had yet to answer for myself. My broken life and broken heart could not withstand superficial family conversation. My heart ached too much to fake it. I wanted to avoid the holidays rather than celebrate them.

Due to my illness, I was unable to work, and the lack of income resulted in listing our home for sale. The self-sufficient security I'd struggle to maintain slipped through my fingers.

Traditionally, our family decorates for Christmas the day after Thanksgiving. However, with all my other losses, I lost the desire to decorate for Christmas. I told my daughter, "Since the house is on the market, I'm not going to decorate as much this year."

Rachel stomped the floor, threw both fists onto her hips, and issued her Grinch of a mother a verbal spanking, "No, Mom! We are celebrating Christmas! Christ's birth! Your Savior's birthday!"

Stunned, my inner two-year-old responded, "Yes, ma'am."

My daughter was right. Regardless of our circumstances, giving thanks is an act of spiritual obedience.

On Thanksgiving morning, my body refused to cooperate. Pain and discomfort seized my skeletal muscles, and I documented the pain as eight out of ten in my medical journal. In the kitchen, I cupped the freshly brewed liquid mercy with both hands, enjoying the heat and the aroma. I pondered the kitchen chalkboard verse, "Give thanks in all circumstances; for this

> Gratitude is the language of heaven.

is God's will for you in Christ Jesus" (1 Thessalonians 5:18). The chalkboard verse gripped my heart. With help from God and Rachel, I chose to celebrate the last Thanksgiving and Christmas in our home. We added extra sparkle to the house that Christmas. I chose thanks *in* my heartache.

Giving thanks is an act of spiritual obedience. Some days, I must purposefully force gratitude because my physical pain automatically generates negative thoughts. Speaking words of thanks and thinking with a positive perspective tethers me to heaven.

Regardless of our circumstance, the Bible encourages us to give thanks in everything. Note that 1 Thessalonians 5:18, does not say give thanks *for* everything but *in* everything. I am not thankful *for* my illness nor *for* my dad's cancer, but I can give thanks *in* our circumstances. I am thankful *in* God's unfailing faithfulness, provision, and peace that no one can explain. I'll be honest, some days the praise doesn't come easy. However, as I offer praise and thanks, God shifts my perspective.

I know my story of holiday stress is not unique. Holiday stress occurs to most Americans. Our society places great emphasis on lavish meals, fancy attire, the more the merrier gatherings, and gift exchanges. The social and cultural aspects of holidays, Christmas in particular, bring unrealistic expectations. Financial strain, anxiety of sharing the kids with the ex-spouse, or walking into a couples' gathering as a single (parent or widow) can be stressful and overwhelming. However, as I offer praise and thanks, God shifts my perspective. Hope does not mean our circumstances change. Hope is resting in Who God is.

 What aspects of the holidays are difficult for you? Have you ever felt the desire to skip a holiday or the hoopla of family functions or fast-forward the calendar? What areas of your life can you say, "Give thanks in all circumstances" (1 Thessalonians 5:18)?

 "Thanksgiving takes the sting out of adversity."

Sara Young, author of *Jesus Calling*[34]

MEET GRACE: SHIFTING FROM DISAPPOINTMENT TO ACCEPTANCE

My senior year in high school was supposed to be perfect. I dreamed it would include tons of friends, laughs, and memories. But God had other plans.

In mid-March 2020, my senior year took an unexpected turn. Concern over the spread of coronavirus canceled scheduled events. Within a short period, administrators canceled our co-op talent show, youth choir fundraiser, and our senior trip to an amusement park. My fear of everything shutting down came to fruition. The school board closed school and implemented online education for the remainder of the school year. The governor banned groups of more than fifty at events in public spaces. No one knew how long this would last. Heartbroken and helpless, I broke down crying after reading my senior year archery season was postponed indefinitely. It seemed everything that could go wrong went wrong. All I could do was stand by and watch my senior year disappear.

There are so many things to learn from the coronavirus situation. I'm learning I should be living every day like it's my last day. I should be treating others in love and trying to make a solid impact for Christ. No one knows how much time they have left on this planet. While having events canceled is not nearly as dramatic as death, it can be symbolic. As I think back on my last archery practice, I ask myself, *did I have a good attitude? Was I Christlike to everyone around me? What will my school remember about me?*

Another thing I'm learning is trust in God. Through all this crazy mess, do I come to Him in anger? Or in complete trust? Can I honestly say that I am okay with my senior year being cut short? An often-quoted verse is Romans 8:28, which says, "And we know that in all things God works for the good of those who love him, who have been called according to His purpose." God's got this. So why are we worried?

The Bible instructs us to praise God in everything, whether good or bad. "Give thanks in all circumstances; for this is God's will for you in Christ Jesus," says 1 Thessalonians 5:18. Give thanks. Praise God because He can see the big picture. God has given us a spirit of love, power, and self-discipline (2 Timothy 1:7). He knows exactly what He is doing, and we should have no reason to fear.

Grace entered her freshman year at Anderson University in the Fall 2020.

RECOGNIZING NEW LIMITATIONS

My active life came to an abrupt halt with the initial attack of full-body paralysis. Like a blown tire forced to move to the side of the road, I watched cars speed past. I used to be on the superhighway of life, and now I was stuck.

As I waited for a tow, in the form of medical intervention, I contemplated my life. I led a rewarding professional career as neighborhood pharmacist. I thrived on face-to-face interaction and dispensing patient care, hugs, and prayers as needed. I enjoyed feeling useful, whether filling a prescription or counseling a patient. At home, my beloved and I are happily married with two children and two dogs; the only thing missing from my American dream life was a white picket fence.

My life, full and active, felt balanced. Working part-time allowed me to keep my pharmacist skills sharp and have time for family, others, and self by retreating to my craft room. When I wasn't working, I stayed busy volunteering at school, participating in a weekly Bible study, serving at church, writing articles, delivering meals, and chauffeuring kids to sports and music lessons. I never stopped.

During initial medical testing, I tried to work, but like a spare tire not intended to travel long distances or more than 50 mph, that notion was short lived. I couldn't keep up with the pace of my job or my previous life. Uncontrollable muscle weakness rendered me unable to open prescription bottles, offer immunizations, or walk. One time, trapped in the pharmacy bathroom, I could not open the heavy metal door. I banged on the door until someone heard my plea for help. I left work in a weak, weepy puddle. Unlike the previous forty years of my life, this illness, I could not control.

During the year I waited for a diagnosis, I stopped being me. I not only exited the highway, but I slowly stopped working, volunteering at my children's school, helping with Vacation Bible School, and attending Sunday school. Self-perseveration became my modus operandi. I came to understand how my body works with this new illness. I learned that on any given day, I could only have enough energy for one activity. I had to preserve me and prioritize my energies. For the first time in my life, I, the pharmacist, took care of me, a full-time patient.

Recognizing my new limitations came with a new sense of guilt. I could not carry on as I had in the past. I joked with friends about having "commitment issues" because plans were always tentative based on how I felt. This also included church. Over time, I discovered that attending Sunday school and church was too much for my body to handle. I desired the company of my church family, but I became quickly exhausted by the attention and conversation. In order to preserve my energy, I attended church service only and often sat in the balcony.

Guilt weighed heavy on my heart when I discussed with my family the changes to our Sunday routine. What were others going to think? Was I letting people down? As the first college graduate on both sides of my family, I wondered if I disappointed my parents. Did God understand? For me, the answer came when reading about David's selection as future king in 1 Samuel 16:7b, "The Lord does not look at the things people look at. People look at the outward appearance, but the Lord looks at the heart."

Slowly, I came to the realization that God knew and cared. This season of pulling back from activities was part of my rest and recovery process. Accustomed to going, doing, and actively participating, I did not know how to rest. I know not everyone will understand this. I am a type-A, got-to-make-a-list-and-get-things-done personality. My friend Bonnie, who battles with fibromyalgia, describes chronic illness as being a stalled racehorse, and I agree with this description.

I struggled with loneliness and isolation. Like Hagar, and many of the Israelites, I too felt abandoned in the desert, but God met me in the dry, parched place of isolation (Genesis 16:13). He reminded me, "I cared for you in the wilderness, in the land of burning heat" (Hosea 13:5). Over the course of the next few years, God taught me to "Be still, and know that I am God" (Psalm 46:10a). He used my illness to reprogram me from a self-sufficient life to a life totally dependent on God. Physically, I could no longer operate as before. Spiritually, I needed to cease striving. I needed to stop thinking that everything would fall apart if I weren't involved. Rest was my word for the year 2018 and Psalm 46:10 was my verse. I needed His sacred rest, not just a nap or a good night's sleep. I needed a desperate reminder that life was not about how much I could accomplish or strive for, but rather how much I was wholly surrendered to God and His will and resting in Him.

 Describe a time when you were forced to pull over. What new limitations did you experience? Thinking back, in what ways did God care for you?

 "Life is very interesting. In the end, some of your greatest pains become your greatest strengths."

Drew Barrymore[35]

BLINKING HAZARD LIGHTS: WHEN WILL SOMEONE NOTICE I NEED HELP?

Suzanne, a divorced single mom, is alone on the weekends when her children are with their father. She posted a question on Facebook asking if Sundays were hard for anyone else. Suzanne pinpointed her need for company when she stated, "On Sundays, when my children are with my ex-husband, I attend church alone and return home to a quiet house. At church, I see people in pairs sitting together, and families going out to lunch after church. It hurts." A plethora of comments followed her Facebook question.

Carla, a married mom of three, responded, "Thank you for sharing this. I wish I lived closer, but you have made me aware of what I need to do to reach out on Sundays." Carla's response drew attention to Suzanne's need for roadside assistance.

At some point, we all need roadside assistance. We need to set down our pride, admit our need for extra assistance, and embrace help when offered. Roadside assistance is necessary when life falls apart. As authors, we understand the dynamic impact of giving and receiving roadside assistance from others who have blazed similar trails before us.

When we notice someone's blinking hazard lights, we need to be the friend who embodies compassion and empathy. Most of us have experienced the desire to help someone during a time of medical diagnosis, loss, or grief. How can we act on our love for others beyond the hollow words and empty offer, "Let me know if I can do anything for you?" What else can we do?

If we look within our own home, we can find unique ways to help others. Those of us who bake can deliver meals to friends in need. Our teenagers can babysit or mow a neighbor's yard. Not only will your neighbor be thankful, but you will also be instilling servant leadership in a generation that needs to see and learn it. If extra time is what is available, consider driving a friend to their cancer treatments. Not only will you enjoy the day with a friend, you will also be giving a much-needed day of rest to their spouse or caregiver. If you possess the gift of organization and administration, then you can organize a Take Them a Meal site, GoFundMe page, or offer to maintain a Caring Bridge website page. Perhaps your gift of words can be used in a call or note. It we take inventory of our gifts, we can be the physical (or electronic) hands and feet of Christ and show His light.

 Who do you know is flashing their hazard lights? What do you have within your house or within your abilities to help? If you're the one in need, don't be afraid to turn your hazard lights on.

 "The friend who loves their neighbor well in trial will continue to come alongside after the initial hardship is over."

Sara Beckman[36]

"We are to pray in times of adversity,
lest we become faithless and unbelieving.
We are to pray in times of prosperity,
lest we become boastful and proud.
We are to pray in times of danger,
lest we become fearful and doubting.
We are to pray in times of security,
lest we become self-sufficient."

Billy Graham[37]

MILE MARKER FIVE

PRESSING ON AND MOVING FORWARD

STEPPING IN THE RIGHT DIRECTION WITH PRAYER

-MARILYN-

Jumping up and down, I try to shimmy into my jeans. I glance in the mirror and think I'm not in the shape I once was. I mumble to myself, *neither is my hair color nor energy.*

TV commercials and Facebook advertisements relay the subtle message, "You're not in good shape and can look better."

In our loss, we want to look better and be better. We want an active life.

If we follow a regular exercise program, we reap other benefits: more energy, less stress, better sleep, and stronger heart and lungs. Even if we don't see dramatic results, we know we feel better physically and emotionally when we exercise. Exercise may even reduce the risk of certain diseases.

Our disciplined exercise becomes a time we look forward to daily. What once seemed like a major effort, we now enjoy because of the positive reinforcement of feeling and looking better. Even though we know the value of exercise and faithfully engage in an exercise program, we may meet an interruption—an illness, an urgent or important event, even a vacation. We miss a day, then three, then give up. We start out strong, but as weeks pass, our motivation fades. We can't even remember the last time we exercised.

Have you thought about the parallels of exercise and prayer? Like exercise, prayer gives us a boost, helps reduce stress, and offers the positive side effect of peace. It strengthens our heart, gives courage when we are stretched by problems, shapes us for what awaits us in our day and week, and boosts our performance. These benefits don't come because requests have been answered, but because we have met with the One Who loves us, hears us, and orders our steps.

Sometimes we're in the same place as the exercise drop-out: we don't pray except for a quick prayer at meals or a few minutes driving. We fade. With exercise, the more we do it, the more we can do and the more we enjoy it. Prayer is the same. When we stay strong in prayer, we can stay strong for each step in our day and the discipline of prayer becomes a delight. Like regular exercise, we feel better when we pray, not because circumstances have changed in the ten minutes we prayed, but because we know our petitions and thanks have been heard. We even look better because our attitude and perspective change and show on our face.

Oswald Chambers said, "Prayer does not fit us for the greater work, prayer is the greater work."[38] We connect with God and get to know Him better each time we pray. Prayer is the greater work for what lies ahead on our routes.

When we face loss, our life changes, and we veer onto unfamiliar paths. We meet new experiences because our loss has altered our route. Some we look forward to as we rebuild; others are stretching; and still some are unknown. Prayer is one way to ask God what He wants us to do to equip us to face the struggles that lie ahead. Prayer is the greater work of preparation.

Jesus knew what was ahead and knew His purpose, but His struggle was still intense. In the garden of Gethsemane, Scripture says He agonized to the point of sweating drops of blood. Yet, He willingly trusted in God's plans. He knew His Father was right—that going to the cross was His purpose in coming—but He was still in anguish. He prayed and walked to the cross knowing He was fulfilling God's plan. When we don't understand what God is doing, especially in our life detours, we can pray with confidence and know His way is always the right way. It may be a long way, a painful way, an inconvenient way, or a hard way, but it is the right way, because it's God's way.

> "Satan dreads nothing but prayer. His one concern is to keep the saints from praying. He fears nothing from prayerless studies, prayerless work, prayerless religion. He laughs at our toil, he mocks our wisdom, but he trembles when we pray."
>
> Samuel Chadwick[39]

The very obstacles keeping me from prayer are the reasons to persevere in prayer. Psalm 9:3 says, "My enemies turn back; they stumble and perish before you." My enemies turn back when I pray and invoke Jesus's name. Jesus used the disciples' sleeping to point out we will fall into temptation. They were exhausted and fell into the natural temptation to fall asleep at a critical time when they could have supported Jesus. In this case, the disciples' enemy was fatigue. Our enemy might be worry, anxiety, jealousy, or comparison, but no matter the enemy, prayer is one way to protect us from wrong thinking, discouragement, and defeat. In our struggle, prayer increases our peace and confidence. As we come out on the other side, prayer guides us to see opportunities and direction.

Today, at the end of my walking routine, I checked my app and read, "2.9 miles, more than yesterday's walk of 2.6 miles." It's one step at a time in the right direction for the exercise program that is right for me. I'm gaining strength and endurance and can fit into my jeans.

Read Matthew 26:36–46. How are your spiritual muscles developing? Is prayer a part of your daily life? If not, pray with me: Dear Lord, I am thankful for Your Sovereign hand on my life. My circumstances are hard, and sometimes, my emotions unravel, but I know You desire good for me. Teach me how to navigate my situation and keep my eyes on You. Jesus, Your name is greater than the name of illness or problem. I trust You. Amen.

"Prayer does not fit us for the greater work, but prayer is the greater work."

Oswald Chambers[40]

CAUTION: BEWARE OF FALLING ROCKS

~MARILYN~

Some people really need to think before they speak. Nearly two years after my husband died, I attended a luncheon and met new friends. As we got acquainted, we shared parts of our stories. When the question arose about marriage, I responded, "I'm a widow. My husband suffered a fatal heart attack two years ago." I gave the Cliff Notes version of his fatal heart attack. This was a social gathering, and I didn't want it to turn into a medical questionnaire or a memorial service.

Without as much as a pause, one woman proclaimed, "My husband had a heart attack three years ago, too, but he survived and is fine. God is so good."

I could not believe the insensitive words that tumbled out of her mouth. *What was she thinking?* Yes, God is good. He is always good. Her husband survived. Mine did not. Does that mean God is good to her but not to me? God's goodness is not dependent on circumstances or outcomes.

Road signs to "Watch for Falling Rocks" dot the landscape of the Blue Ridge Parkway. The same stones used to build the bridges and overpasses have the potential to tumble down the mountainside. The same is true with words. The words we speak possess the power to build up or tear down. Like stones skillfully selected for building, our words, if chosen correctly, can lift one another up. The perfect word rooted in Biblical truth can provide God's perspective during any crisis. However, we need to beware of falling rocks—senseless or sharp words that tumble and block the path of healing for others.

King Solomon, known as the wisest person in the Old Testament spoke this proverb, "The tongue has the power of life and death" (Proverbs 18:21a).

{ God's goodness is not dependent on circumstances or outcomes. }

The Apostle Paul tells us to speak only words that will benefit and build others up. "Do not let any unwholesome talk come out of your mouths, but only what is helpful for building others up according to their needs, that it may benefit those who listen" (Ephesians 4:29).

Most of us have heard the story of Eve's deception. Satan is the father of lies. He has no new skills. He uses the same tactics of lies, doubt, and deception about God that he always uses. He modifies them where needed to assault us in our vulnerable places. He did this in the form of a serpent, when he questioned Eve, "Did God really say?" (Genesis 3:1). While we might not fall for that trick, we need to be aware of other sly questions he might convey such as, "If God loved you, He wouldn't allow _____ to happen." He might say, "God can't forgive what you did. Hasn't God let you down? Your life won't change. It will always be like this. Why didn't your husband survive? Why did you lose your job? Why do you have this diagnosis? Does God really love you?" When we buy into those lies, we become disillusioned or discouraged; we stop praying and reading His Word. We begin to distrust God.

At the luncheon, I had a choice. I could stumble over the rocks of insensitive words and pick them up in my mind for days, hurting myself, or I could take them to Christ. Again, Paul reminds us what to do. "We demolish arguments and every pretension that sets itself up against the knowledge of God, and we take captive every thought to make it obedient to Christ" (2 Corinthians 10:5). We need to beware of falling rocks and if they fall move them with God's strength.

So, let's not be "that woman." Are the words we say building up or tearing down? Before we speak THINK. Is what we are about to say True? Helpful?

Inspiring? Necessary? Kind? And think, how you would receive the words you speak?

 How did you handle the last time someone wounded you with words? What would you do differently? What comes to mind when you read, "Take captive every thought to make it obedient to Christ" (2 Corinthians 10:5)?

 Before we speak, THINK. Is what we are about to say True? Helpful? Inspiring? Necessary? Kind?

MAKING SENSE OF SETBACKS AND DISAPPOINTMENTS

Are you struggling to make sense of setbacks and dealing with disappointment? Maybe you can relate to Tammy who posted on Facebook, "Today is my thirty-second wedding anniversary, my third anniversary without my husband." She goes on to say that, as a widow, she is not celebrating in a usual fashion, rather she is reminiscing in sorrow, over the missed years and memories. Perhaps you've been part of this scenario. A friend pulls out her phone to display their family's beach photos. Jealousy strikes. Waves of disappointment crash because your financial setbacks make that trip impossible for you.

In her book *Faith Enough to Finish*, Jill Briscoe reminds us that God's goal is to fashion us into a work of art. Yes, our disappointments and setbacks are real. They hurt and might immobilize us for a while, but Briscoe reflects, "God used the circumstances of life to shape me. Undoubtedly the chisel of disappointment and loss and of shattered dreams and broken promises played their part." Jill recounts, "In the plan of God, problems can be a platform for God."[41]

A platform? Yes, we can use our struggles to make God famous. When we have struggles but not solutions, we can stand in His grace. When life takes a turn that knocks us over, we can display His strength to get up each day.

Tennis star Serena Williams uses her platform to encourage female athletes and moms everywhere. Ten months after the birth of her daughter, Serena Williams returned to the court and fell short of winning her twenty-fourth Grand Slam. Not surrendering to defeat, she peered into the stands and addressed the crowd, "To all the moms out there, I was playing for you today. And I tried." As a mother and fierce competitor, she understands disappointment and setbacks.[42] Perspective is crucial. Serena Williams says, "I've grown most not from victories but setbacks. If winning is God's reward, then losing is how He teaches us."[43]

April didn't imagine her temporary medical leave of absence was a set up for medical retirement. "Little did I know when I climbed over the guardrail of safety and security (my plan) and stepped off a cliff (into God's plan), I would free fall into His grace. Sometimes, it is only the insight of hindsight that allows us to make sense of our setbacks. It took me over four years to understand this concept. While I still ponder His plans for my future, I can praise God for His presence in my messy life.

> I get by every day with Jesus, coffee, and afternoon naps.

"I'd like to say I've overcome all my hang-ups, but I haven't. I still struggle with my identity as a stay-at-home-mom, rare illness warrior, writer, and forced-into-retirement pharmacist. I wish I could tell you I no longer struggle with my current situation or my illness. But I can't. Most days I feel like a stalled racehorse eager to run a race, only to discover I don't have the energy to get out of the gate. This illness forces me to rest daily. I get by every day with Jesus, coffee, and afternoon naps.

"God continues to teach me how He wants to use me for His kingdom, plans, and purposes, none of which include serving as the local pharmacist. With the insight of hindsight, I see these perceived setbacks were actually a set up for God to work in me and through me."

We can turn to God in our setbacks and disappointments. God is big enough to handle our tears, questions, and temper tantrums. According to Jeremiah 29:11, God has plans and we have a future. "'For I know the plans I have for you,' declares the Lord, 'plans to prosper you and not to harm you, plans to give you hope and a future.'" God has the plans and we do not. We have a future with Him. We have hope.

In what areas are you struggling to make sense of setbacks and dealing with disappointment? Is prayer your first response or last resort? How does Philippians 2:13 encourage you: "For it is God who works in you to will and to act in order to fulfill his good purpose"?

"In the plan of God, problems can be a platform for God."

Jill Briscoe[44]

MEET NICKI: LETTING GO OF CONTROL AND TRUSTING GOD'S PLAN

I had my life planned since childhood. I would attend Word of Life Bible Institute after high school then graduate from Liberty University. I would teach first grade, marry the love of my life, and deliver five children (I already had their names chosen). Looking back, I can see how arrogant I was to plan my future and expect God to bless my wishes.

After college, I moved to a new town. I sat in a church pew every Sunday and cried. Actually, I cried almost every day. Years of feeling inadequate in multiple areas of life caught up with me. I was depressed and felt hopeless.

I always had a strong desire to be married and have a family and felt it was my life's calling. But I was in my twenties with no signs of a relationship on the horizon. I was angry and disappointed with God. Even though deep down I knew God is good, I questioned the truthfulness of that statement for me. My life certainly didn't seem good at the time, (because it wasn't going according to my plan). I knew God wanted me to surrender my desire to be married and have children to Him. What He really wanted was for me to believe life with Him was enough. Surrendering my hopes and dreams to the Lord was a real struggle.

Proverbs 19:21 says, "Many are the plans in a person's heart, but it is the Lord's purpose that prevails."

It took me a long time to surrender. I wanted things my way. I thought I could only be satisfied if I had the fulfillment of marriage and children. But God showed me He is a good Father, and I can trust Him. I struggled and pleaded with the Lord for years, but ultimately, I came to the knowledge that He is enough. Once I surrendered my desires, I met my husband, and we were married a year and a half later.

Since my husband and I were married later in life, we knew we wanted to have children right away. A few months after we were married, doctors informed us that my husband could not father a child. My husband had brain cancer as a child. The radiation treatment, which saved his life, made it impossible for him to father a child. I was devastated. Once again, I had to surrender my dreams to the Lord. This was another big challenge. My identity was emotionally attached to my dreams, but God helped change my thinking. Instead of thinking about what I was giving up, God helped me to embrace the One whose will I was choosing. I gained Christ's perspective. I trusted God's plans are always better than my own.

I thought surrender meant we would not have children, and I was learning to accept that decision. But God blessed my meager trust as only He can. It began with a conversation in 2018 in my second-grade classroom. My students asked why I didn't have children. I explained that my husband and I couldn't get pregnant.

Immediately they piped up, "Mrs. Dietz, you are like Sarah in the Bible!" (We had just studied the story of Sarah and Abraham.) Then they said, "Let's pray right now that God gives you a baby! It will be your Christmas miracle!"

Oh, the faith of a child! I had been so focused on surrendering my dreams of children to the Lord I hadn't even thought He would make another way. Because of my students' prayer, I too I began to pray for a baby. Then God burdened my heart for adoption. When I told my husband, I thought God might want us to adopt, he said God was telling him the same thing! We began the journey and God did the work.

I felt confident in my ability to be a mom; however, the idea of adoption shook my confidence and pushed me closer to Christ. I learned to trust Christ and His enablement instead of myself. That is a freeing place to be! The entire process of adoption was overwhelming, but I stepped out and asked the Lord to give me faith to trust Him. When we learned the average cost of private adoption is $30,000, God gave us faith to believe He would provide. When matched with an infant girl whose birth mom used drugs and who had no prenatal care, God gave us faith to believe He would heal this baby. When our baby girl arrived seven weeks prior to her due date with all the funding raised, God continued to grant us faith. We even had money left over to aid in the hotel costs and additional out-of-pocket expenses from our baby's extensive NICU stay.

The prayers of my second-grade class came to fruition. Our adopted Christmas miracle was bundled in pink, and because of the generous gifts of God's people, we had no outstanding bills from the adoption process. So many people, many of whom are strangers to us, covered our baby in prayer.

Each time I made the sacrifice of surrender, God blessed tremendously. There is pain in releasing and offering our good plans to God, but God is a good Father who gives good gifts to His children, in His timing and in His way. We can trust Him.

Now, fifteen years later, I sit in the church pew and I praise God. A few tears slip down my cheeks, but they are mostly tears of thankfulness and worship. Does that mean that life is perfect? No. Did my plans work out? Not exactly the way I had planned. But life is good and most of all, God is good!

LEARNING CONTENTMENT

I am still adjusting to the stay-at-home-mom gig. I commend those who make the choice to stay at home their top priority, but it was never part of my plan. Nor was the unexpected illness that put me here. My unexpected journey required numerous adjustments. The adjustment from a dual income to a single income resulted in the downsizing our home (to one-level wheelchair accessible), our children leaving private school, and completely re-shifting financial priorities. Though I am several

> "I have learned how to be content whatever the circumstances."
> Philippians 4:11b

years into my new role, I thought I would have adjusted to my new gig by now. But honestly, I still struggle.

During the transition to our new home in 2017–2018, I read *The Resolution for Women*, by Priscilla Shirer. Per her instructions to readers, I scribed these words on an index card and attached it to the front of my fridge.

> "I do solemnly resolve to embrace my current season of life and will maximize my time in it. I will resist the urge to hurry through or circumvent any portion of my journey but will live with a spirit of contentment."—Priscilla Shirer, *The Resolution for Women*[45]

Contentment is a new skill I'm learning to develop. Like any new skill, it requires frequent repetition, trial, and error. The first summer in our new home, our neighbor excavated their backyard to make way for an in-ground pool. I am embarrassed to admit the stinkin' thinkin' thoughts that welled up. Thoughts such as, *Oh great, we have to sell our lake house and our neighbors have the money for a pool.* I had to take these thoughts captive to Christ (2 Corinthians 10:5) and practice contentment. As the bulldozers excavated their backyard to make room for a pool, God excavated my heart to make room for contentment. I had to choose to let go of life's disappointments and learn the new skill of contentment. Why? Disappointment points to lack; whereas contentment turns what we have into enough. Now I recognize, we live in a great neighborhood and we adore our neighbors. In fact, we have two neighbors with pools and an open invitation to swim anytime.

More than being content to swim in my neighbor's pool, I had to learn to practice the skill of contentment with what I had, where God had led me, and what was ultimately in my hands. This required God's tender compassionate bulldozer to excavate my fragile heart. These verses resonated in my heart during this time of gentle excavation:

"For the eyes of the Lord range throughout the earth to strengthen those whose hearts are fully committed to him" (2 Chronicles 16:9a).

"Whatever you do, work at it with all your heart, as working for the Lord, not for human masters, since you know that you will receive an inheritance from the Lord as a reward. It is the Lord Christ you are serving" (Colossians 3:23–24).

{ Contentment turns what we have into enough. }

Overwhelmed by all the changes in our lives, I recited this daily prayer, "Lord, find me faithful. Amen." This simple prayer allowed me to keep focused on honoring God with what was in my hands, rather than comparing myself to what others were doing or what resources they possessed. As a racehorse is fitted with blinders, the prayer, "Lord find me faithful," served as my spiritual blinders to keep me focused on what God called me to do.

During my season of learning contentment, I discovered two Bible passages where people felt ill-equipped and unqualified in their roles.

For seven years God allowed the Midianites and others to invade the Israelite's land because "The Israelites did evil in the eyes of the Lord" (Judges 6:1). Midianites, Amalekites, and other eastern peoples invaded the land like swarms of locusts. These enemies ravaged the land, ruined the crops, and stole the Israelites' livestock. God chose to answer the Israelites' plea for help by using an unlikely person: Gideon, the weakest in his clan. An angel of the Lord called Gideon a "valiant warrior" and instructed him to fight the enemy. God saw in Gideon what Gideon didn't see in himself—a source of strength in God. "Go in the strength you have" (Judges 6:14). Reluctantly obedient, Gideon and his motley crew of a few defeated a large enemy in an unexpected way.

Armed with the strength given by God, he first took care of matters at home. Gideon cleaned house and destroyed his father's images of false gods. The townspeople were in awe of such a defiant act, but they realized that if Gideon was still alive, then the false gods were no gods at all. Gideon moved in God's power, not his. Perhaps this first act gave Gideon confidence and prepared him for bigger battles. Another passage in Scripture tells us to not despise small beginnings because it is there that God begins his work (Zechariah 4:10).

Judges chapters 6–8 chronicles the defeat of a large army by Gideon's few men who were all acting in God's power. As I read, my weak self was encouraged. If God could give strength to Gideon, He could do the same for me.

The second influential passage was 2 Kings 4:1–7, where I met an unnamed recent widow. Left with debts she cannot repay, the debt collectors threatened to take away her two sons. Desperate, she pleads to the prophet Elisha for help. Instead of helping, he asks, "What's in your house?" She confesses to having only a little oil. Elisha instructs her to gather as many jars as she can from the neighbors. (Can you imagine the humility of having to ask the neighbors for help?) Elisha blessed what little oil she had, and the oil miraculously continued to pour until all the jars were full. Using what she had—her jars and her voice to ask for help—she was able to sell the oil, pay off her debts, and keep her sons.

Gideon and the unnamed widow viewed themselves as weak and ill-equipped, but God saw their potential and He honored their obedience. As we look at our losses and life-altering situations, we may feel weak and ill-equipped. But God gives strength, uses our availability, and honors obedience. Sometimes we have to clear our thinking, like Gideon cleared his father's house. Perhaps we need to swallow our pride and ask for help or use what we have in our house. But above all, we need to rest in God's power to do what He asks where He places us.

As shown in the stories of Gideon (Judges 6) and the widow (2 Kings 4:1-7), what is God calling you to do in His strength? How can you use what you already have to bless others? Write 2 Corinthians 12:9 on an index card and keep it handy for encouragement.

"Gratitude turns what we have into enough."

April White

GLANCING IN THE REARVIEW MIRROR

-MARILYN-

My high school driving instructor held a sheet of paper up to the rearview mirror and asked what was behind me. I had just glanced a few seconds earlier, so I knew it was a blue car.

"Great job!" he said. "You paid attention."

When bruised by a brutal blow, we are tempted to gaze in our rearview mirrors. We remember what life was like before our "incident"—when we held hands with the love of our life, answered the door for a Friday night date, were healthy, had a career, earned a paycheck, or cradled a child. We reminiscence, wishing life could return to the way it was.

Staring out our rearview mirror is normal; however, as a new driver, my instructor told me to glance, not linger or focus. If I did the latter, I would surely swerve off the road or get in an accident. In life, I can glance back and remember the people and experiences who were a part of my life with love and gratitude. But that is not where I live.

Glancing in the mirror reminds me of God's faithfulness. Remembering how He provided for me in the past will strengthen my faith in how He will provide now. God's character is faithfulness. Like the sunrise, His mercies and kindness arrive each day. His promises tell me they will show up today. He keeps His promises. We glance in rearview mirrors for reminders and safety, but we don't focus there. Keeping our eyes on the road and maintaining the right speed is the only way to move on in our new path. That's where I'm going.

-APRIL-

For many, Thanksgiving is a day steeped in gratitude, family, and pumpkin pie. For me, however, Thanksgiving Day triggers memories of my former self. It is a day of mourning for the person I was before my chronic illness.

As soon as my son was old enough, we ran in the Drumstick Dash. The Drumstick Dash is a 5K fundraiser for the Roanoke Rescue Mission held on Thanksgiving morning. My husband and daughter would walk the 3.1 miles, stopping at Texas Tavern for a bowl of chili, but Andrew and I raced to the finish line in an attempt to beat the previous year's personal best. Running was an activity we both enjoyed. I loved this annual mother-son experience.

Four Thanksgivings have passed without our family's participation. I miss the cold morning meeting in downtown Roanoke, seeing friends, their families, and the crazy dressed runners. I miss the annual T-shirts. I miss being physically strong and independent. But most of all, I miss my old self, the one who didn't know about Hypokalemic Periodic Paralysis, much less wear a medical alert bracelet with the diagnosis.

Time has helped heal my broken heart. However, waves of nostalgia crash on the surf of my heart leaving fragments of memories of life before the illness. During these moments, I give myself grace to respect the process, but I do not allow myself to wallow there.

We've all heard the cliché, "Be careful what you ask for," and I confess it is true. A few years before my illness, I set out to learn more about the writing craft. Until this point, I wrote regularly for my blog, Red Chair Moments. But my posts were random and lacked strategy and consistency. With the encouragement from friends, I registered for the Blue Ridge Mountains Christian Writers Conference. In May 2015, I attended this conference apprehensive and alone, but I left the conference empowered and with dozens of new friends. When I returned to my day job, as a pharmacist, all I wanted to do was write. My reoccurring prayer was this, "Lord, please give me more time to write. Time that doesn't take away from my family."

God has a sense of humor. He answered the above prayer but in an unpredictable fashion. The method He chose is called Hypokalemic Periodic Paralysis. Each day, I wake up to an answered prayer. Now I have plenty of time to write that does not take away from my family. I may not have plenty of energy, but I asked for time and God granted me time. I realize God is predictably unpredictable. And so are His ways. "For my thoughts are not your thoughts, neither are your ways my ways,' declares the Lord" (Isaiah 55:8).

Like Marilyn, I glance back at my old life and grieve it, but I cannot linger there. Marilyn and I are both learning to fix our eyes on Jesus, the Author and Perfecter of our faith (Hebrew 12:2). We know He is writing new chapters in our lives.

 A glance in the rearview mirror of God's past faithfulness during difficult times will strengthen our resolve for our present and future needs and changes. Write examples of when God showed you His faithfulness. Don't hurry through this activity, but let your heart dwell here. God is a promise keeper. What promise from the Bible are you clinging to right now?

 "Fixing our eyes on Jesus, the pioneer and perfecter of faith. For the joy set before him he endured the cross, scorning its shame, and sat down at the right hand of the throne of God."

Hebrews 12:2

REENTRY: MERGING BACK INTO SOCIETY

-MARILYN-

The best advice I received after the death of my husband was to "Grieve in the way that is right for you. Grieve your way and on your timetable." At some point, though, we must learn to merge back into life, and the pace of this reentry process is as unique as the individual.

There is no suggested speed or way to merge back into life after a crisis. In his book *Shattered Dreams,* Larry Crabb shares two unwritten rules that surface in response to hurting people. "First, mourning has a time limit. Second, we think there is a proper way to mourn. Ugly battles should remain out of sight. Acceptable battles may be shared, but only if we season our account with hope . . . where the real story is never told, the power of God is not felt."[46] How long does it take to overcome? It takes as long as it takes. But those unwritten rules are not true: mourning doesn't have a time limit and there is no universal way to respond to your loss. Our grief and response to crises are as unique as our fingerprints. There are no cookie cutter plans for overcoming a crisis and merging back into society. Adjustment and mourning lasts as long as they last.

The stages of grief, which include denial, anger, bargaining, depression, and acceptance, operate on their own agenda without the constraints of time. Developed for people facing a terminal illness, there are no neat timelines. The phases of grief are different. They ebb and flow like the ocean tide. Days, weeks, and months are different (better?) then waves of grief enter without notice. Even years later, you might have a grief burst. I cried one day baking my mother's recipe. I envisioned her in our kitchen, standing over her Mixmaster and memories flooded my soul. That day was forty-five years after her passing. Memories and incidents, watching a familiar movie you watched with your love years ago, trigger thoughts and bring tears. My friend Martha recounted, "Sometimes I break down in tears just because the wind changed direction." A familiar smell, sight, or an event can trigger a time with our loved one and tears flow. One of my projects while sheltering in place during the pandemic was sorting old slides and photos. Some brought smiles and others a visual of the exact place and date, with people now gone, causing tears to well up.

Reentry is the process of merging back into society. This isn't like merging back into traffic after pulling over to eat at Cracker Barrel or returning to work from vacation and wearing the new outfit you bought. Merging back into society is accompanied by hardship and a new perspective with a desire to return to a normal (ha!) way of life. Yes, it is new but hardly normal.

I reviewed my journals as I wrote this piece. Seriously, some of those days remain a blur. A counselor who spoke at a grief support group said that God designed it that way. If we thought clearly in early grief, we'd collapse at the reality of the situation. So as I turned pages in my journals, I read:

> January 17, 2012: I led my small group Bible study in my home on the names of God. What a stark change in my life. I'm clinging to His character in His names.

> January 25, 2012: I can pray more than a few words aloud without tears.

> January 2012: I'm attending a grief group to get tools to manage my new life.

> March 26, 2012: My fourth month without Randy. It is hard to believe. My heart hurts. God has stayed close to me everyday.

Waiting is what I do now, directing my attention to what He says is next. For the moment, it is "stand still."

May 2012: I'm preparing for my daughter Kate's wedding and relying on God's strength to be fully present for her big day. My word from Exodus 9:16, "But I have raised you up for this very purpose, that I might show you my power and that my name might be proclaimed in all the earth." God continues to meet me where I am.

December 2012: I hired a painter. Now three rooms have new colors. My home changed, and now the connection of Randy in my house has changed too. What will life be like when I relocate?

During this time, I continued to ask God, "What's this all about?" And in my spirit, He continued to respond, "Trust me."

Life interruptions present a different normal, a new script, different scenes, and different people who come and go. Not only are we re-entering, we are remodeling and rebuilding. It takes time and strength. Six months after Randy passed, my youngest daughter married and relocated. I had no family in the area. The few steps forward I made in those six months didn't stop a new swell of grief; a grief of being alone in an area without family. Two-and-a-half years later, I said goodbye to a loving church family and neighbors who were my best friends and relocated to a new state to be near family. Secondary losses were front and center as I made major solo decisions. The heaviness of the shifting pronouns from "our" to "my" was a boulder on my chest as I met people and used the singular pronoun.

Secondary losses are other losses and changes due to the primary loss. These secondary losses may be unrecognized by others, because they are unaware or they are personal in nature, but these secondary losses affect the griever in real ways. Every morning my husband kissed the top of my head and we drank coffee together. I miss both. In my widowhood, I eat alone in a quiet house, while pondering how to handle the responsibilities of yard work, home repair, and car maintenance. Not to mention the finances and taxes Randy maintained. With each year and new experience, a secondary loss comes, such as the birth of a grandchild he was not present to hold.

My path is a process of knowing (and reminding myself) Who God is and relying on His steadfast character.

> "You have searched me, Lord, and you know me. You know when I sit and when I rise; you perceive my thoughts from afar. You discern my going out and my lying down; you are familiar with all my ways. Before a word is on my tongue you, Lord, know it completely. You hem me in behind and before, and you lay your hand upon me. Such knowledge is too wonderful for me, too lofty for me to attain."
>
> Psalm 139:1–6

How perfect He had prepared me by studying the names of God. Although I had suffered a major change, I could ride the waves of grief and pain with His provision. As I read Psalm 139, I remind myself nothing comes as a surprise to Him, even the degree to which I hurt.

I reentered and rebuilt my life in a way and time that was right for me. My greatest comfort emerged from relying on God's truth, a dear widowed friend who mentored me, reading books and articles relating to grief and widowhood, and the consolation of faithful friends who connected with me in practical ways. However, in daily living I learned to take initiative. I also learned:

- When invited to participate in certain activities, I gained courage to say either, "Yes, Let me think about it," or "No thanks" without giving a reason.

- When attending a gathering, I learned to drive separate rather than carpool, so I could leave when I was ready to leave.

- To leave lights and music on so I wouldn't return to a dark and quiet house.

- Not to expect people, who have not experienced my pain, to understand my life-altering grief and loneliness and to give them grace.

- Some friends leave, but God will send new friends who are tailor-made for my new season.
- To appreciate the investment of time and encouragement other widows made in me and to now do the same for others.
- Strength comes when I need it, not before, so don't practice anticipatory anxiety.
- To take breaks from social media for my own mental health.
- If I want to thrive I need to move forward—maybe in baby steps, maybe big steps.
- I don't need to apologize for tears, declining invitations, or saying I miss my husband.

There is no universal timetable for mourning and reentry. Only yours. Keep in mind the road you're on is full of mental road signs: caution, reentry, remodeling, and rebuilding. In the delays, rest stops, and construction ahead, stand in grace and God-confidence. There is always a sign in view that says, "HOPE."

-APRIL-

In the early years of my illness, I played a mental game of tug-o-war: purpose versus productivity. The gap between realistic and unmet expectations contained a lot of frustration for me. One day my fried Sara said, "April, you don't have to be active to be productive."

Our society equates busyness with importance. Our social media driven world pushes for "likes" and "followers." However, these superficial numbers don't equate to true relationships or success. Society confuses busyness and productivity with importance and success. Society applauds the wonder woman mom who can juggle many plates and not break any, while leaving the struggling mom on her own. Our culture has programmed us to rely on self instead of relying on God. God issued a programming guide of six days of work and one day of rest, and relying on God means taking advantage of the rest He's given us.

With the help of medications, physical therapy, and counseling, I learned how to alter my expectations to accommodate my change in circumstances. I tell friends, "I have commitment issues." While I say this in honest jest, it is true. On most days, I have enough energy for one activity a day, and I survive each day with Jesus, coffee, and afternoon naps. During this time, I also stepped away from serving at church and school. In lieu of having a dedicated role in Vacation Bible School, I volunteered on the days I felt good and served behind the scenes.

Merging requires a true self-assessment of our current situation, abilities, strengths, and needs. Merging back into society requires slow and deliberate yielding with extra margin of time and rest.

What is your experience with merging back into society? What adjustments did you make and what new changes do you need to add? What choices do you no longer make?

"Our success is not measured by how much we get done—it's measured by whether we trusted God in days that feel totally unproductive."

John Piper[47]

COUNT YOUR BLESSINGS. RECOUNTS ARE OKAY

-MARILYN-

Who knew a jar filled with slips of paper could hold extraordinary treasures? I once heard a story of a family's nightly routine of thankfulness. They wrote what they're thankful for on slips of paper and placed them in a jar. At the end of the month, they dumped the papers out and remembered God's gifts.

I knew this practice of gratitude would guide my focus in the right direction. Instead of emptying the jar each month, I saved it for the first Christmas morning I would spend alone. When Christmas day arrived, my heart longed for past Christmases filled with children's laughter and girlie chatter. I missed our family tradition of matching pajamas and my husband videotaping our gift opening on Christmas day. We would open our gifts, one at a time, and with five people, it took an entire morning. Sons-in-law added to our family, followed by grandchildren and more excitement and matching pajamas for all. During these gatherings, I always said, "My cup runs over."

With a warm cup of coffee and a slice of my traditional cherry bread on a Christmas plate, I dumped my jar and read each one as God's gifts to me that year. Each slip of paper was a reminder of God's faithfulness—extraordinary everyday treasures, my pink peonies, a FaceTime call, holding my grandson. These gifts were not store bought but were handcrafted by my God who loves me.

It is easy to count our blessings in times of prosperity, when life is good, when the kids are behaving, and when we have more money than month. But what about during a drought, a global pandemic, when your teen is caught smoking weed, or when money is tight? In the Old Testament, the prophet Habakkuk said if the fig tree didn't bloom, and if there were no olives or grapes, he would still rejoice in God (Habakkuk 3:17–19). It is during these hard times when we need to count our blessings; recounts are okay.

> "Gratitude gets us through the hard stuff. To reflect on your blessings is to rehearse God's accomplishments."[48]

Paul instructs us to "Give thanks in all circumstances; for this is God's will for you in Christ Jesus" (1 Thessalonians 5:18). He does not instruct us to be to be thankful *for* but *in*. We are not thankful for a chronic illness or the death of a loved one but *in* remembering that God promises to "never leave you nor forsake you" (Deuteronomy 31:6). We are not thankful for a prodigal child but for consolation *in* God's principle that if we "start children off on the way they should go, and even when they are old they will not turn from it" (Proverbs 22:6).

Whatever trial we are facing, we can express our gratitude for what we are learning, His provision of friends, refinement of our character, new opportunities, the comfort of others, and the presence of God. We can give thanks as we look at the distance we have covered in our new journey with His grace, His wisdom, and His guiding hand. In a society that focuses on counting steps, counting calories, and counting money, instead count and recount your blessings.

That Christmas morning, I was thankful I had a different view. Oh my house was painfully quiet. The laughter of children from long ago was absent. I missed my husband's voice and presence. There were no husband/wife gifts under the tree, but I did have my gift of gratitude for God's blessings. My cup ran over.

Take a moment to count your blessings. Jot them down on a slip of paper as a visual reminder when your spirits feel low. Consider taking this lesson a step further by starting your own gratitude jar or gratitude journal.

"Sometimes God may prioritize performing a miracle on our hearts and minds over a miracle concerning our circumstances."

Beth Moore, *Believing God*[49]

"Life can only be understood backwards; but it must be lived forwards."

Soren Kierkegaard[50]

MILE MARKER SIX

PULL OVER AND
ADMIRE THE VIEW

TRUSTING GOD'S TIMING

Our family of four tucked into the couches with popcorn, soda, and snuggly blankets for a family movie night. We chose the 1971 classic *Willy Wonka and the Chocolate Factory* as our evening entertainment. My favorite character in the movie is the spoiled and bratty Veruca Salt, who is famous for stomping and demanding, "But I want an Oompa Loompa now!"[51]

Veruca Salt's rotten behavior triggered the memory of a telephone conversation in the early weeks of my short-term disability. I mentioned this conversation in my earlier story, *Wrestling with God*. My friend Meg phoned to check on me. I told her, "I'm halfway through my paid short-term disability. God has six more weeks to figure out what's wrong with me so I can 'name it, claim it, and move on.'" As soon as those words left my mouth, I was aghast. Had I really mimicked and stomped like Veruca Salt to God? I knew I was wrong when I demanded "to know what is wrong with me right now."

Waiting and trusting in the Lord feels intolerable at times. I am guilty of allowing my impatience in God's timing to flare. I am guilty of misbehaving like Veruca Salt as I stomp around and voice brazen demands to my loving Father. Disgusted by my prideful bratty attitude, I stopped and asked for forgiveness and the strength to wait for God's timing.

On New Year's Day 2016, I wrote out the word TRUST vertically on a note card. Beside each letter, I scribbled as many words as I could think of that began with that letter. By the end of this brainstorming session, I created my personal definition of TRUST.

Truly

Rely on God's

Unfailing

Sovereign

Timing

For me to trust God, I must truly rely on God's unfailing sovereign timing, which means I must totally surrender my notion of control. Truly trusting God means we nap in the back seat of the car, rather than demanding our own way, reaching for the steering wheel, or offering unsolicited directions. It has taken years for me to become a backseat napper rather than a backseat driver.

Jesus took time for a nap. Matthew, Mark, and John wrote the story of Jesus and His disciples encountering a major storm. The disciples were frantic and were surprised to find Jesus napping in the back seat of the boat, with a pillow! Jesus, Who is all-knowing, knew about the storm before He stepped into the boat. He rested in His Father's care and watchful eye. He commanded, "Be still," and the storm ceased.

> "Be still and know that I am God."
> Psalm 46:10

As followers of Christ, we are to watch, listen, and behave like Jesus. This account of Jesus napping during a raging storm is an example for how we should behave. Trust in God is the only way to possess this level of peace and rest during the fiercest of storms.

In her book, *One Perfect Word*, Debbie Macomber chronicles stories of God's hand in her life each year when she intentionally focused on one word.[52] In 2016, I claimed "trust" as my word for the year. Throughout the year, I scoured God's Word and wrote out every verse that contained the word "trust." As a result, I chose Romans 15:13 as my verse for the year, "May the

God of hope fill you with all joy and peace as you trust in him, so that you may overflow with hope by the power of the Holy Spirit." I left 2016 with a personal definition of the word "trust." For me, to trust God means I must truly rely on God's unfailing sovereign timing.

Our willingness to participate in an archeological dig in God's Word helps us find buried treasure specific to our situation. God's Word is active and alive, sharper than any two-edged sword. God will reveal a special verse at a specific time for a specific person. Answers develop over time by careful examination of the native language, root words, and historical context. We see other verses that complement our word or verse. We cannot rush this excavation process or we will miss the details. Just as prayer is a discipline, so is daily reading God's Word. We don't use a checklist or make it into a task, but a deep desire to read God's love letter to us.

Consider exploring one word, phrase, or verse for an extended period. Perhaps, the area in which you struggle the most should be the area of greatest excavation. If God has radically altered the trajectory of your plans, He desires to walk alongside you and deepen your faith every step of the way. Dig for what He wants to show you.

Acronym for TRUST:

Truly

Relying on God's

Unfailing

Sovereign

Timing

April White

MEET ANGIE: RECEIVING PEACE DURING INCARCERATION

How do you find peace when all is lost? How do you find peace when you can't change your circumstances? These are the questions I wrestled with while serving eight years in prison.

My mental image of peace usually involves water—walking beside a tranquil stream, sitting on the dock at the lake, or soaking up the sun by the ocean while wiggling my toes in the sand. It's easy for me to find peace in those beautiful places where things are going well and life is good.

But how do you find peace when life is the worst it has ever been? How do you find peace in the middle of the storms? How do you find peace when you've lost everything—your home, your career, your father, and your freedom? How do you find peace when you can't be with your child, when you are unable to protect and guide her as she grows up? When you know you are missing her life and the celebrations and struggles? How do you find peace when people have failed you and you even feel like God has abandoned you?

The answer is, humanly, you don't.

The reality is there is nothing you can do to find peace. You have to go to the water—the living water. Jesus told the woman at the well, "If you knew the gift of God and who it is that asks you for a drink, you would have asked him and he would have given you living water" (John 4:10).

Did you hear that? *"He would have given."* Jesus gives the water. He *is* the living water. In the twenty-third Psalm, David writes, "He leads me beside still waters. He refreshes my soul" (Psalm 23:2b–3a). That sounds like peace to me. He leads. He restores. Christ says in John 14:27, "Peace I leave with you."

There is nothing I can do to find peace. I sit and God gives it.

It makes no sense that I am able to put aside my sadness, worry, and fear to sleep through the night on a metal bed in this terrible place but I can. Paul, who also understood prison life, wrote in Philippians 4:6–7: "Do not be anxious about anything, but in every situation, by prayer and petition, with thanksgiving, present your requests to God. And the peace of God, which transcends all understanding, will guard your hearts and your minds in Christ Jesus."

The keywords from Paul's script are "prayer" and "peace of God." Every night when I lie down, I pray and recite Scriptures until I fall asleep. When I am too overwhelmed by emotions and I can't seem to pray, I know that my brothers and sisters in Christ are praying for me and that Jesus Himself is interceding for me, and rest eventually comes. "In peace I will lie down and sleep, for you alone, Lord, make me dwell in safety" (Psalm 4:8).

The world defines peace as a state of tranquility, quiet, and harmony; freedom from disquieting or oppressive thoughts or emotions. The prison in which I am forced to live for now is not a place of peace. It is a place of self-centeredness, anger, resentment, noise, conflict, disrespect, foul language, and nasty attitudes. It is very hard to feel peaceful here.

But true peace has nothing to do with your circumstances, your environment, or your feelings. Peace is a gift from the Holy Spirit. It's the quiet assurance in your soul that God is in control; He's got you in the palm of His hand from your first breath to your last.

So, if you are looking for peace—stop and ask.

The Holy Spirit freely gives us His peace, and we must shoe our feet with that peace so that we can stand firm against the attacks of the enemy and walk forward in faith.

READING THE OWNER'S MANUAL

-MARILYN-

My heart raced as I adjusted my seat behind the steering wheel of my new car. My salesman sat in the passenger seat and explained each knob, button, and light on the dashboard. The new buttons and gadgets overwhelmed me, but the salesman reassured me that I didn't have to memorize everything because the information was in the owner's manual. I was thankful for written information. After my crash course, he took my photo to send to my family. As I drove off the lot, I prayed I'd made the right decision and reminded myself if anything went wrong, I had an owner's manual.

I've often reflected on my new car purchase experience and the spiritual parallel it offers. Wouldn't it be convenient if every decision had plain direction and a black and white answer? If we had answers to our why, how, and when questions? If we could snap a photo to share, showing everything worked out just fine?

Well, all of us have an owner's manual.

God's owner's manual, the Bible, provides instructions and guidelines related to daily living and decisions. Pages of Scripture describe faithfulness on a difficult path, comfort in pain, wisdom for choices, and the high cost of disobedience. We also read of the beautiful mercies and unending forgiveness of God. But unless we read and study, we won't know God's mind and heart. We won't know His promises of comfort or faithfulness in hard times. We can look at what a passage means, but we also ask, how does it apply to me?

{ "We just have to realize how crucial it is to get into God's Word and have His Word get into us . . . I think it is God's mercy to prepare you today for what you'll need one day. It may be something complicated coming your way. Or something hard. Or even a blessing that He needs to prepare you for. Whatever it is, God's Word is your lifeline. When instruction from God's Word is what we heed, we are more able to discern His direction for what we need." }

Lysa TerKeurst[53]

-APRIL-

God's Word is "a lamp for my feet, a light on my path" (Psalm 119:105). If we want to travel well and see our path and who God wants us to become, His Word is what we need to grab on to every day. What may start as an obligation to read, with time, will become a delight as you see the Author is in your presence waiting for you to open His book.

August 9, 2016, a concoction of anxiety, curiosity, and hope, pulsed through my veins as I prepared to attend an 8:00 am appointment (my first appointment) at Duke Medical Center. My husband and I drove three hours to Raleigh, North Carolina, the night before and stayed at our friend's house. I vividly recall standing at the kitchen counter, cupping a mug of freshly brewed liquid mercy and reading through Isaiah. A passage of Scripture I had read hundreds of times before leaped off the page: "With deep compassion I will bring you back" (Isaiah 54:7b).

I wept when I read this passage. God's promise to bring me back was enough. But for God to bring me back, restore me with compassion . . . well, as we say in the south, y'all, I was a hot mess. God knew. He knew precisely what my heart needed to read and at the right moment. Isaiah 54:7 is circled and marked with the words "8/9/16 Before Duke Appt." written in the margin. This promise is a placeholder in my heart, a reminder to remember God's faithful words.

God is bringing me back. He is restoring me both spiritually, mentally, and physically. Spiritually, He continues to teach me to surrender control (which is difficult for a type-A planner personality) and to truly trust in Him even when nothing makes sense. Mentally, I am learning to change my perspective from negative to positive and to recite the words of *Brilliant Perspectives* speaker, Graham Cooke, "I am not a sick person. I am a well person, fighting off a sickness."[54] Physically, I am able to somewhat manage my illnesses with the help of medication, an autoimmune diet (AIP), and a careful balance of rest and activity. Some days are better than others, some hours are better than others. But overall, I get by with Jesus, coffee, and afternoon naps.

 When have you wanted an owner's manual for your specific dilemma? Do you have a pattern of regular Bible reading and study? There are many print and online devotions to help you develop and maintain a habit. Some people like to read the Bible in a year or take the book of Proverbs and read one a day. Another idea is to read the book of Psalms. Pray about your approach to checking your owner's manual for optimum maintenance.

 "When asked, 'What is more important: praying or reading the Bible?' I ask, 'What is more important: breathing in or breathing out?'"

Russ Scalzo[55]

PREPARING FOR THE UNEXPECTED

-APRIL-

My daughter crisscrossed her legs and tucked her ankles under her bottom. Rachel flipped through her stack of vocabulary flash cards and moaned, "Mom, can you email the teacher and ask what the test will be like? Will it be multiple choice?"

"Nope."

"Please," she begged.

"Rachel, you need to know this information backward and forward. If you know in advance your test is multiple choice, you will study only to recognize the answer. You need to know this information inside and out. You need to be prepared no matter how you are tested."

As soon as I uttered that last sentence, the Holy Spirit nudged me; not a tangible nudge, but rather a nudge in my spirit. *You need to be prepared no matter how you are tested.* Were those really my words to begin with, or did the Holy Spirit plant those words in my mind to speak to me via Rachel? Either way, those words penetrated my soul with a deeper significance than my daughter's upcoming vocabulary test.

Are you ready for your test?

The fact is that each one of us will face a test in life. Sometimes we have ample time to prepare, such as launching young adult children to college or transitioning aging parents into an assisted living facility. Other times, tests strike like a bolt of lightning in a pop-up summer thunderstorm, such as an unexpected health diagnoses, the death of a loved one, an accident, separation, or job loss. Blindsided and dazed, these sudden storms wreak chaos and confusion to those of us seeking immediate shelter. Where we seek shelter in the storm will determine our perspective and our progress. During the COVID-19 pandemic, we sheltered in place. Social media and conversations revealed our complaints and impatience with the situation at hand. But there were also comments showing gratitude for the newfound time at home with family and a slower paced life.

The good news is that God's Word gives us detailed instruction on how to prepare for the tests and pop quizzes of life. Get your pencils ready.

Six Ways to Prepare for the Unexpected Test:

1. Seek: "Look to the Lord and his strength; seek his face always" (1 Chronicles 16:11). (Also, see Jeremiah 29:13, Deuteronomy 4:9, Psalm 27:4, Psalm 119:2, Isaiah 55:6, Lamentations 3:25, Hebrews 11:6, and Matthew 7:7.)

2. Abide/ Remain: "Remain in me, as I also remain in you. No branch can bear fruit by itself; it must remain in the vine. Neither can you bear fruit unless you remain in me" (John 15:4). (Also, see Exodus 33:14, Psalm 92:12–15, 2 Corinthians 5:7, John 16:33, John 15:7–10.)

3. Surrender: "For whoever wants to save their life will lose it, but whoever loses their life for me and for the gospel will save it." (Mark 8:35). (Also, see Isaiah 64:8, Psalm 37:7, Mark 10:28, Matthew 16:24–25, Galatians 2:20, Romans 12:1.)

4. Obey: "You are my portion, Lord; I have promised to obey your words" (Psalm 119:57). (Also, see Luke 11:28 Psalm 119:88, 168, Ecclesiastes 8:5, Matthew 8:27, John 14:23–24, Romans 2:13.)

5. Trust: "When I am afraid, I put my trust in you" (Psalm 56:3). (Also, see Hebrews 6:19, Psalm 20:7, Isaiah 26:3, Proverbs 3:5, Psalm 37:3, Psalm 44:6–7, Jeremiah 17:7, Isaiah 26:4.)

6. Pray: "Therefore confess your sins to each other and pray for each other so that you may be healed. The prayer of a righteous person is powerful and effective" (James 5:16). (Also, see 1 Thessalonians 5:16–18, Matthew 6:6-9, Matthew 5:44, Matthew 26:41, Luke 22:40, Romans 8:26.)

Tests look different and meet us throughout life. We have either passed through a trial, are in one, or will face one in the future. So, I often hold review sessions and remember God's truths. In college, I studied Organic Chemistry much the same way I study the Bible. With colorful index cards, I drilled the chemical structures into my brain. Now, I use colorful index cards to drill spiritual structures—Bible verses and encouraging quotes—into my brain. I must remind myself of God's faithfulness in the past, present, and future.

Security and God's provision is under constant review in my life. Sticky notes with verses dot the landscape of my bathroom mirror and kitchen cabinets. My well-worn and well-loved Bible contains penned marks in the margins indicating where God met me in that particular time in my life.

> "A Bible that's falling apart usually belongs to someone who isn't."
> Charles H. Spurgeon[56]

I recognize I am no longer the one in control of my income and my health. My years of training and education as a pharmacist allowed me a comfortable lifestyle. Our family followed Dave Ramsey's Financial Peace University plan and made wise financial choices. We weren't rich, but we could always afford to eat steak. The illness that hijacked the plans for my life actually launched me to a front row seat of God's provision. Without the ability to work (as the primary wage earner of our family), I was forced to rely on God. Don't get me wrong, my husband earns a good salary with his career, but the loss of my income forced us to make drastic decisions and reach back to what we've been taught about God.

Think about a recent test. Which of the six ways to prepare for an unexpected test stand out as an area to explore? What is holding you back from digging deeper with God? What are you afraid to find?

"If God sends us on stony paths, He will provide strong shoes."

Corrie ten Boom[57]

HIDE-AND-SEEK

-MARILYN-

"Ready or not, here I come!" ricochets though the house. My grandchildren love to play hide-and-go-seek. The seeker searches under beds, in closets, and behind trees for the hidden friend. It's fun for kids, but when adults play, it takes on a different meaning.

Carolyn relates to hiding. She battled prescription drug addiction for twenty years. Domestic abuse compounded her physical pain. As the violence increased, so did her pain, and the cycle of drug abuse continued. "My turning point came when I was arrested for a DUI. I knew it would happen eventually. While incarcerated for sixty-eight days, my husband of forty-two years suddenly died. In the beginning, I received limited support from my family until I proved I was serious about getting help. That's when I found and entered a faith-based recovery house for women with addictions."

> "When you go through a trial,
> the sovereignty of God is the pillow
> on which you lay your head."
> Charles Spurgeon[58]

Carolyn is now free from both physical and substance abuse. She drew closer to God and found worth in Christ Jesus. Today, she shares her story with women who are victims of substance and domestic abuse.

God does not waste the painful chapters of our lives. We can't delete them like a computer file, but we can use them as examples of God's redemption. With transparency, we don't have to hide, but we can seek.

By seeking God's face, both in prayer and in Bible reading, we can know He is a safe place to hide. We will find refuge when life falls apart. Seeking the face of God teaches us to remember His character traits. As we mentioned in "You Expect Me to Sing Here?" if we memorize the attributes of God, we can cling to His character and promises in a season of disruption.

> "My heart says of you,
> 'Seek his face!' Your face,
> Lord, I will seek."
> Psalm 27:8

Throughout Scripture, God invites us to hide-and-seek with Him. "God is our refuge and strength, an ever-present help in trouble" (Psalm 46:1). In His refuge, God provides hope, comfort, and the strength to carry on.

Another key component of seeking is pursuing the guidance of others who've walked similar paths. Engaging the wise counsel of a friend or a professional counselor provides a depth of clarity we miss. Carolyn went to a place of healing with a plan. "I knew self-help and willpower was obviously weak or hadn't worked nor did encouragement from family. I needed something more. I had more to deal with than an addiction for prescription drugs, but also scars from domestic abuse I endured most of my married life. The God-centered program included church attendance. I started going to church and received unconditional love and support from my Life Group. Bible study set me on the right track. I saw hope and a new life was possible as the director lived in sobriety for over fifteen years. My circle of friends and family understood the severity of the abuse, but their empathy didn't solve the problem." Often our nearsightedness blurs perspective. Mentors or those with spiritual insight, practical recommendations, and maturity can offer wise counsel to help us see clearer.

In addition, God desires to incorporate our past hurts into healing for others. C. S. Lewis, author of *The Chronicles of Narnia* observed, "Friendship is born at that moment when one person says to another: 'What! You, too? I thought I was the only one.'"⁵⁹ Sharing our story with transparency can provide hope for others.

God designed us to live in community not separate islands. Our story is part of a grander picture to help others. God can turn our messes into messages and our tests into testimonies. We must first recognize our need for help and look beyond ourselves. God can meet us where we are.

Shame and isolation are the enemy's tools to keep us in hiding. Shame and isolation can be either self-inflicted or arise from the words and actions of others. Satan would prefer we hide behind a mask rather than be real with our hurts and weaknesses. He doesn't want us to share our stories or ask others to pray for us. He knows someone may have a solution for our plight, be a mentor, guide us in the right direction, or faithfully pray for us. He knows there is power in prayer, that communicating with the One Who created us will sustain us and will meet our needs. As we stumble in hard times, we need to seek God's face. When we hide in His shelter, He finds us, but we are the winner.

"But if from there you seek the LORD your God, you will find him if you seek with all your heart and with all your soul" (Deuteronomy 4:29).

What distracts you or keeps you from praying or reading Scripture? Do you wrestle with doubts or disappointments that God won't be enough?

"Those who know your name trust in you, for you, Lord, have never forsaken those who seek you."

Psalm 9:10

MEET KATHY: REDEEMING THE LOSS OF A CHILD

Kathy knows loss is sometimes forever. "On July 1, 2007, our son-in-law killed our twenty-five-year-old daughter Tonia. Her death is a forever loss. Shock, numbness, mind-blowing grief happened in the minutes, hours, and days after her death. Our daughter's death has changed who we are and who we continue to become. Unless it happens to you, no one understands the emotions surrounding losing a child. The death of a child leaves so many voids. There are many layers to loss. There is a loss of the future you once planned, future grandchildren, and future special events you share together. There is a loss of the traditions around holidays and birthdays. There is a loss of sibling relationships."

Kathy offers these thoughts when grieving the loss of a child:

- Surround yourself with people who have already walked this journey.
- Give yourself more time than you think you need to do the heavy lifting of grief. Grief is for a lifetime. You will never get over it. But the pain lessens with time.
- Know that even years later, you will have periodic bursts of grief, like waves from a storm, flood your heart.
- Do not be afraid to get professional counseling to aid in your journey. You may feel guilty the first time you laugh but know that it is okay to laugh, sing, dance, and feel joy in your life.
- Communicate your wishes on how to remember their birthday and the anniversary date of their death. Ask friends to talk

about your loved one, share memories, and use their name. It's important to know others have not forgotten your loved one. Let them know they won't make you cry by bringing up a memory.

- For married couples, your grief will affect you differently than your spouse. Your communication will need to change. Give grace to your spouse and ask for grace from them. This takes time, patience, and love. Reach out to other couples who have learned and who are thriving despite the loss of their child. Take care of yourself so you can care for the rest of your family.

Kathy says her faith was her biggest gift. "I have grown to know God in deeper ways. I can take my struggles to Him. I may never understand why Tonia died, but I trust God is in control. For the first time in my life, I have learned to trust God completely. God has become my pillar of strength in the darkness."

As a result of her daughter's death, Kathy is involved in Umbrella Ministries for grieving parents. She and her husband are also active in a marriage ministry where they focus on presenting God's design for marriage and pouring into hurting marriages.

"Our story echoes to a hurting world. Tonia's death has opened many doors for us sharing Who God is and how He can help in your time of sorrow and pain."

You can find more about Kathy Brundage's story in the resources.

GO IN THE STRENGTH YOU HAVE

I teetered to the mailbox, thankful for the strength to walk that far. Two doors down I caught a glimpse of my neighbor who was returning home from his afternoon walk. Usually his wife of over sixty-years joined him; however, she was home recuperating from a recent surgery.

I should visit, I thought as I pivoted my weight and regained my balance on the wooden post. After all, Southern hospitality dictates that I deliver a meal. However, I struggled to walk much less possessed the energy to cook. A verse from story of Gideon resurfaced, "Go in this strength you have" (Judges 6:14). I pondered the significance of this verse while my mother's mantra echoed in my ears, "April Dawn, sometimes you got to make do with what you have until you can do better."

I knew mom was right. Armed with a pair of scissors and a reused canning jar, I took inventory of my backyard blooms. I snipped crimson roses, mint, magenta butterfly blossoms, and sunny yellow African lilies. My simple homegrown backyard bouquet was all I had to offer.

Armed in the strength I had, God's provision of strength in me, I slowly walked two doors down. I carefully grasped the glass jar with both hands. Peripheral neuropathy caused my hands to go numb while nerve endings buzzed and crackled. At first, I was hesitant to visit because I had nothing special to offer. I had no grand meal prepared, no cookies baked, not even a card, but my neighbor was thrilled with the surprise visit and backyard bouquet.

I thought all I had to offer was a humble backyard bouquet, but as I walked home, I realized I overlooked the greatest gift I have—the gift of myself. We should never underestimate giving our time and friendship to others.

What comes to mind with the phrases "Go in the strength that you have" or "What is in your house?" How can you bless someone today with what you have?

"Goodness is the only investment that never fails."

Henry David Thoreau[60]

SENDING YOU OUR FAREWELL POSTCARD OF HOPE

For each of us, life will not be without changes, challenges, and losses. Though you may look back from time to time on your notes in your travel diary about lessons learned, know that ultimate rest is found in finding and pursuing a relationship with Jesus Christ. He pursues us like the lost sheep as demonstrated in Luke 15:3–7 and loves us enough to die a sacrificial death on a cross for each one of us (John 3:16).

He is our Ultimate Rest Area, and we offer this postcard to you:

> "Come to me, all you who are weary and burdened, and I will give you rest. Take my yoke upon you and learn from me, for I am gentle and humble in heart, and you will find rest for your souls. For my yoke is easy and my burden is light" (Matthew 11:28–30).

Thank you, courageous friend, for traveling with us. We trust you arrived at these last pages with a greater sense of hope and confidence in God and with the knowledge that you are not alone.

Together, we've covered much ground. Perhaps you have lingered at some areas longer than others. Maybe certain mile markers were roadblocks where you stopped to sort your next steps. As you continue to live and move in the land of hope, we leave you with these reminders for your journey:

Jesus Never Leaves nor Forsakes Us (Hebrews 13:5)

- Jehovah-jireh will provide in unexpected ways, often different from what you expect.

- Friends leave or betray us, perhaps uncomfortable by our change in circumstance or feeling like we no longer fit in their circle or their narrow-minded scope of friendship.
- Other friends press in and love like never before.
- Jesus brings new friends, with compassion and warmth, who understand our situation.

God Has a Plan—Trust Him (Jeremiah 29:11)

- God is not surprised by our dilemma.
- He makes all things new—including you—in this trial.
- God is not mad at you. He loves you.
- This process is painful, but He is excavating your heart, digging to the root. He desires to strengthen your foundation so He can rebuild and restore.

Keep Your Eyes Fixed on Him During the Process (Hebrews 12:1)

- Dwell in His Word.
- Pray without ceasing.
- Spend time with others who have walked similar paths, not to commiserate, but for mutual encouragement and understanding.
- Know that time spent in prayer and in the Word will radiate joy.
- Read this book, devotions, listen to podcasts, songs.
- Saturate yourself daily in truth and hang on for dear life.

You Will Get Through This (Isaiah 43:2)

- Hang on to His promises.
- God calls you an overcomer, a faithful warrior.
- You have a unique story of God's deliverance, redemption, and provision. Share your story with others; someone needs to hear it.

- He wants to deliver you from your insecurity so that you can fully rely on Him; keep your focus on Him, not your loss or circumstances.
- Lean in, seek, and be empowered by God's unfailing faithfulness. In Him, there is hope.

MILE MARKER SEVEN

APPENDIX, RESOURCES, AND BIBLIOGRAPHY

APPENDIX

Packing Scripture A-to-Z

Consult your map, pack appropriately, and travel with real hope.

A. "When I am **afraid,** I put my trust in you" (Psalm 56:3).

B. "The **battle** is not yours but God's" (2 Chronicles 20:15).

C. "**Cast** your **cares** on the Lord and he will sustain you" (Psalm 55:22).

D. "So do not fear, for I am with you; do not be **dismayed**, for I am your God. I will strengthen you and help you; I will uphold you with my righteous right hand" (Isaiah 41:10).

E. "I will **exalt** you, Lord, for you lifted me out of the depths" (Psalm 30:1a).

F. "For the Spirit God gave us does not make us timid (**fearful**), but gives us power, love and self-discipline" (2 Timothy 1:7).

G. "But he said to me, 'My **grace** is sufficient for you, for my power is made perfect in weakness.' Therefore I will boast all the more gladly about my weaknesses, so that Christ's power may rest on me" (2 Corinthians 12:9).

H. "So we say with confidence, 'The Lord is my **helper**; I will not be afraid. What can mere mortals do to me?' (Hebrews 13:6).

I. "In the same way, the Spirit helps us in our weakness. We do not know what we ought to pray for, but the Spirit himself **intercedes** for us through wordless groans" (Romans 8:26).

J. "For the **joy** of the Lord is your strength" (Nehemiah 8:10).

K. "Teach me **knowledge** and good judgment, for I trust your commands" (Psalm 119:66).

L. "Your word is a **lamp** for my feet, a **light** on my path" (Psalm 119:105).

M. "Set your **minds** on things above, not on earthly things" (Colossians 3:2).

N. "The **name** of the Lord is a fortified tower; the righteous run to it and are safe" (Proverbs 18:10).

O. "Through Jesus, therefore, let us continually **offer** to God a sacrifice of praise—the fruit of lips that openly profess his name. (Hebrews 13:15).

P. "Not only so, but we also glory in our sufferings, because we know that suffering produces **perseverance**; perseverance, character; and character, hope. And hope does not put us to shame, because God's love has been poured out into our hearts through the Holy Spirit, who has been given to us" (Romans 5:3–5).

Q. "He makes me lie down in green pastures, he leads me beside **quiet** waters" (Psalm 23:2).

R. "Come to me, all you who are weary and burdened, and I will give you **rest**. Take my yoke upon you and learn from me, for I am gentle and humble in heart, and you will find **rest** for your souls. For my yoke is easy and my burden is light" (Matthew 11:28–30).

S. "God is our refuge and **strength**, an ever-present help in trouble" (Psalm 46:1).

T. "**Trust** in the Lord with all your heart and lean not on your own understanding; in all your ways submit to him, and he will make your paths straight" (Proverbs 3:5–6).

U. "Let the morning bring me word of your **unfailing** love, for I have put my trust in you" (Psalm 143:8).

V. "I am the **vine;** you are the branches. If you remain in me and I in you, you will bear much fruit; apart from me you can do nothing" (John 15:5).

W. "**Wait** for the Lord; be strong and take heart and **wait** for the Lord" (Psalm 27:14).

X. "Finally, brothers and sisters, whatever is true, whatever is noble, whatever is right, whatever is pure, whatever is lovely, whatever is admirable—if anything is **excellent** or praiseworthy—think about such things" (Philippians 4:8).

Y. "Take my **yoke** upon you and learn from me, for I am gentle and humble in heart, and you will find rest for your souls" (Matthew 11:29).

Z. "Desire (**zeal**) without knowledge is not good—how much more will hasty feet miss the way" (Proverbs 19:2).

TRUTH STATEMENTS

Continued from: Who Told You That? Debunking
Lies and Recalculating Thoughts

- A valiant warrior (Judges 6:12).
- A secret weapon in God's army (Isaiah 49:2).
- Not afraid of evil for God is with me (Psalm 23:4).
- Capturing negative thoughts and making them obedient to Christ (2 Corinthians 10:5).
- Being transformed by the Potter into something He deems best (Jeremiah 18).
- A princess or prince to the Most High King (2 Corinthians 6:18).
- Clothed in God's armor (Ephesians 6:11).
- More than a conqueror (Romans 8:37).
- Seated in heavenly places with my Father and King (Ephesians 2:6).
- Actively listening for my Father's voice each day during my #CoffeeWithJesus (John 10:27).
- Chosen by God (Ephesians 1:4).
- Loved by God (John 3:16).
- Forgiven by God (1 John 1:9).
- Sustained by God (Psalm 119:116).
- Strengthened by God (1 Peter 5:10).
- Led by God (Psalm 23).
- Secured by God (Psalm 16:8). *This is April's life verse.
- Blessed when I come and blessed when I go (Deuteronomy 28:6).

RESOURCES

Kathy Brundage is the author of *From Homicide to Healing*, available for online purchase at www.lulu.com/spotlight/KathyBrundage. More of Kathy's story can be found at www.rememberingtonia.wordpress.com. You can learn about Umbrella Ministries/Sisters of Hope at www.sistersofhope-richmond.com.

Dorothy Deming is a speaker for women's groups and shares her story at these online locations: www.intrainingministries.org, Facebook: @intrainingministries, Twitter: @intraininmin.

Nan Jones is an author/speaker who uses the words of her heart to assist fellow Christians discover the presence of God in their darkest hour. Her book, *The Perils of a Pastor's Wife*, was a 2016 Selah finalist and her blog, *Beyond the Veil*, won first place in the Foundation Awards at the 2017 Blue Ridge Mountains Christian Writers Conference. Nan is a contributor to *Inspire a Fire*, inspirational blog, and a weekly program producer of *Beyond the Veil* on Hope Stream Radio. When Nan isn't writing, she enjoys leading prayer retreats, teaching Bible studies or sharing God's faithfulness as keynote speaker for special events. Visit Nan's website: www.NanJones.com or her Facebook ministry page, Seeing Beyond The Veil. Contact Nan at nan@nanjones.com. *The Perils of a Pastor's Wife* is available on Amazon and Barnes and Noble.

Erin Odom is the author of *More Than Just Making It: Hope for the Heart of the Financially Frustrated* and *You Can Stay Home with Your Kids: 100 Tips, Tricks, and Ways to Make It Work on a Budget*. Visit her website, www.TheHumbledHomemaker.com, where you can also purchase her books.

BIBLIOGRAPHY

1   Lewis, C.S. *The Four Loves.* New York, NY: Harcourt Brace Jovanovich Publishers, 1960.

2   Wilson, Neil. *Lonely Planet: Scotland.* London, England: Lonely Planet Publishing Group, 2015.

3   Lucado, Max. *You'll Get Through This: Hope and Help for Your Turbulent Times Nashville.* TN: Thomas Nelson Nashville, 2013.

4   "What is Periodic Paralysis?" Periodic Paralysis International. Submitted June 21, 2011. https://hkpp.org/what-is-periodic-paralysis.

5   Spafford, Horatio G. "It is Well with My Soul." Public Domain. 1873. http://www.songsandhymns.org.

6   Kingsley, Emily Perl. "Welcome to Holland." 1987. http://www.our-kids.org/Archives/Holland.html.

7   Frankl, Viktor E. Accessed July 8, 2017. https://www.brainyquote.com/quotes/viktor_e_frankl_121087.

8   Jones, Nan. *The Perils of a Pastor's Wife.* Raleigh, North Carolina: Lighthouse Publishing of the Carolinas, 2015.

9   Blanchard, John. *Discovering God: 365 Daily Devotions.* Carol Stream, IL: Tyndale House Publishers, Inc., 2015.

10 "Wikipedia: Corrie Ten Boom." Wikimedia Foundation. Last modified November 24, 2020. https://en.wikipedia.org/wiki/Corrie_ten_Boom.

11 "The History of the Museum." Corrie Ten Boom House. Accessed October 26, 2020. https://www.corrietenboom.com/en/information/the-history-of-the-museum.

12 Rothschild, Jennifer, *Psalm 23 - The Shepherd With Me.* Nashville, TN: LifeWay Press, 2013.

13   Gregory, Christina. "The Five Stages of Grief: An Examination of the Kubler-Ross Model." PSYCOM. Last updated Sep. 23, 2020. https://www.psycom.net/depression.central.grief.html.

14   Coke, Graham. "The Lord is Our Keeper." *Brilliant Perspectives*. Published March 12, 2019. https://brilliantperspectives.com/the-lord-is-our-keeper.

15   Emerson, Ralph Waldo. Quote Fancy. Accessed July 8, 2017. https://quote-fancy.com/quote/893532/Ralph-Waldo-Emerson-Not-in-his-goals-but-in-his-transitions-man-is-great.

16   Groeschel, Craig. *Altar Ego: Becoming Who God Says You Are*. Grand Rapids, MI: Zondervan, 2013.

17   Powell, Enoch. Brainy Quote. Brainy Media Inc. Accessed July 8, 2017. https://www.brainyquote.com/quotes/enoch_powell_159642.

18   Frost, Robert. "Stopping by Woods on a Snowy Evening," in *The Poetry of Robert Frost: The Collected Poems, Complete, and Unabridged*. New York, NY: Henry Holt and Company, Inc., 1979.

19   Hopwood, James Jeans. Goodreads. Accessed July 8, 2017. https://www.goodreads.com/author/show/7500730.James_Hopwood_Jeans.

20   "Picture Quotes." Lessons Learned in Life. Published August 31, 2017. https://lessonslearnedinlife.com/be-thankful-for-the-stall/.

21   Lewis, C. S. Brainy Quote. Brainy Media Inc. Accessed May 1, 2020. https://www.brainyquote.com/quotes/c_s_lewis_714973.

22   Spurgeon, Charles. Goodreads. Accessed November 25, 2020. https://www.goodreads.com/quotes/1403154-god-is-too-good-to-be-unkind-and-he-is.

23   Sills, Beverly. *Bubbles: A Self-Portrait*. New York, NY: Macmillan Publishers, 1976.

24   Story, Laura. Instagram. Published November 18, 2019. https://www.instagram.com/p/B5A9DP2prdt.

25   Story, Laura. The Bargain Hunter. Published October 8, 2019. https://the-bargainhunter.com/news/arts/ohio-star-theater-welcomes-laura-story-in-concert.

26   Barrie, J.M. What's Your Grief. Accessed April 29, 2020. https://whatsyour-grief.com/wp-content/uploads/2015/02/Barrie.jpg.

27   Winfrey, Oprah. Brain Quote. Brainy Media Inc. Accessed April 24, 2020. https://www.brainyquote.com/quotes/oprah_winfrey_105255.

28   Furtick, Stephen. Facebook. Published September 6, 2018. https://www.facebook.com/watch/?v=322642158283907.

29   Author Unknown. *Chicken Soup for the Soul.* Simon & Schuster Digital Sales Inc., 2015.

30   Koning, Otto. *The Pineapple Story.* 2004; Oakbrook, IL: IBLP Publications. Audio CD.

31   Ibid.

32   Morris, Robert. Published on April 29, 2020. https://www.instagram.com/p/B_lFnc3F81b.

33   Humphrey, Hubert H. Brainy Quote. Brainy Media Inc. Accessed July 8, 2017.https://www.brainyquote.com/quotes/hubert_h_humphrey_152600.

34   Young, Sara. *Jesus Calling: Enjoying Peace in His Presence.* Nashville, TN: Thomas Nelson Publishers, 2004.

35   Barrymore, Drew. Brainy Quote. Brainy Media Inc. Accessed July 8, 2017. https://www.brainyquote.com/quotes/drew_barrymore_129676.

36   Beckman, Sara. *Alongside: A Practical Guide for Loving Your Neighbor in the Time of Trial.* Newport News, VA: Morgan James Publishers, 2017.

37   Graham, Billy. "5 Quotes on Prayer from Billy Graham." The Billy Graham Library (blog). August 28, 2017. https://billygrahamlibrary.org/5-quotes-on-prayer-from-billy-graham.

38   Chambers, Oswald. *My Utmost for His Highest.* Grand Rapids, MI: Discovery House Publishers, 2012.

39   Chadwick, Samuel. Goodreads. Accessed November 25, 2020. https://www.goodreads.com/author/quotes/1148687.Samuel_Chadwick.

40   Ibid.

41   Briscoe, Jill. *Faith Enough to Finish.* Mansfield, TX: Monarch Books, 2007.

42   Creech, Jenny. "Serena Williams An Inspiration to Moms Everywhere." Houston Chronicles, July 6, 2019. https://www.houstonchronicle.com/sports/columnists/dialcreech/article/Serena-Williams-an-inspiration-to-moms-everywhere-14076172.php.

43   Goalcast. "Top 20 Serena Williams Quotes to Inspire You to Rise Up and Win." Goalcast.com, August 8, 2017. https://www.goalcast.com/2017/08/08/top-20-serena-williams-quotes-to-inspire-you-to-rise-up-win.

44 Briscoe, Jill. *Faith Enough to Finish.* Mansfield, TX: Monarch Books, 2007.

45 Shirer, Priscilla, Kendrick, Stephen, and Kendrick, Alec. *The Resolution for Women.* Nashville, TN: B& H Publishing Group, 2011.

46 Crabb, Larry. *Shattered Dreams: God's Unexpected Path to Joy.* Colorado Springs, CO: Waterbrook Publishers, 2012.

47 Piper, John. Twitter. Published March 11, 2018. https://twitter.com/johnpiper/status/972990585681469445?lang=en.

48 Lucado, Max. *You'll Get Through This: Hope and Help for Your Turbulent Times.* Nashville, TN: Thomas Nelson, 2013.

49 Moore, Beth. *Believing God.* Nashville, TN: B&H Publishing Group, 2006.

50 Kierkegaard, Soren. Brainy Quote. Brainy Media Inc. Accessed July 8, 2017. https://www.brainyquote.com/quotes/soren_kierkegaard_105030.

51 Dahl, Roald. *Willy Wonka and the Chocolate Factory.* Directed by Mel Stuart. Los Angeles: Paramount, 1971.

52 Macomber, Debbie. *One Perfect Word.* New York, NY: Simon and Schuster, 2013.

53 TerKeurst, Lysa. *Trustworthy: Overcoming Our Greatest Struggles to Trust God.* Nashville, TN: Lifeway Press, 2019.

54 "Q & A with Graham Cooke: Living in physical pain while walking in the grace of God." Youtube. Posted on March 4, 2019. https://www.youtube.com/watch?v=ApyO92yPcjs.

55 Scalzo, Russ. Goodreads. Accessed November 25, 2020. https://www.goodreads.com/quotes/5369244-when-asked-what-is-more-important-praying-or-reading-the.

56 Spurgeon, Charles. Sermon Quotes. Accessed November 2, 2020. https://sermonquotes.com/authors/charles-spurgeon/8507-bible-thats-falling-apart.html.

57 Ten Boom, Corrie. Goodreads. Accessed April 8, 2016. https://www.goodreads.com/quotes/518158-if-god-sends-us-on-strong-paths-we-are-provided.

58 Spurgeon, Charles H. Quote Fancy. Accessed May 8, 2018. https://quotefancy.com/quote/785357/Charles-H-Spurgeon-When-you-go-through-a-trial-the-sovereignty-of-God-is-the-pillow-upon.

59 Lewis, C.S. *The Four Loves.* New York, NY: Harcourt Brace Jovanovich Publishers, 1960.

60 Thoreau, Henry David. Goodreads. Accessed November 25, 2020. https://www.goodreads.com/quotes/94470-goodness-is-the-only-investment-that-never-fails.

COMING SOON!

- *Destination Hope: A Devotional Companion When Life Falls Apart*
- *Destination Hope: Thirty-one Days of Prayers for Your Journey*
- Extras and freebies: Downloadable graphics from our websites

We love to hear from our readers. Please connect with us on our websites and on social media, www.MarilynNutter.com and www. AprilDawnWhite.com.

Warmly,

Marilyn and April

Ambassador International's mission is to magnify the Lord Jesus Christ
and promote His gospel through the written word.

We believe through the publication of Christian literature, Jesus Christ and
His Word will be exalted, believers will be strengthened in their walk with
Him, and the lost will be directed to Jesus Christ as the only way of salvation.

For more information about
AMBASSADOR INTERNATIONAL
please visit:

www.ambassador-international.com

*Thank you for reading this book. Please consider leaving us a
review on your social media, favorite retailer's website,
Goodreads or Bookbub, or our website.*

Separation is difficult to understand, to cope with. But after experiencing a painful separation herself, Mollie is well-equipped to help others work through this time. *Hopelessly Hopeful During Separation* is a devotional written to encourage others to use their time of separation to grow closer to God.

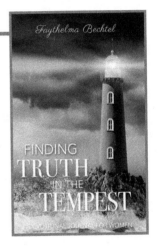

As we walk through dark times in our lives, we all need a way of *Finding Truth in the Tempest*. Faythelma Bechtel knows the tempest, but she also knows the One Who calms the storm. After losing two daughters and her husband, Faythelma has clung tighter to her Savior and longs to help others who are struggling to find peace in their own storms. This devotional journal is not meant to be read as a daily plan, but instead offers meditations on Scripture to help for your unique circumstance.

We all have something that keeps us from living fully for the Lord, but Christ wants us to give our baggage to Him so we can follow Him freely. In *Pack Your Baggage, Honey, We're Moving to Paris!* Anne Farnum explores the different kinds of baggage we carry. She also focuses on the baggage that King Saul hid behind and compares it to that which David left behind to run toward the giant.

CPSIA information can be obtained
at www.ICGtesting.com
Printed in the USA
LVHW081604280921
698925LV00014B/678

9 781649 601094